T0115287

WHAT WOULD THE
BUDDHA
RECYCLE?

A Mindful Guide to an
❧ Eco-Friendly Life ❧

Adams Media

New York   London   Toronto   Sydney   New Delhi

A **adams**media

Adams Media
An Imprint of Simon & Schuster, Inc.
57 Littlefield Street
Avon, Massachusetts 02322

This Adams Media hardcover
edition November 2020

ADAMS MEDIA and colophon are
trademarks of Simon & Schuster.

For information about special
discounts for bulk purchases,
please contact Simon & Schuster
Special Sales at 1-866-506-1949 or
business@simonandschuster.com.

The Simon & Schuster Speakers Bureau
can bring authors to your live event. For
more information or to book an event
contact the Simon & Schuster Speakers
Bureau at 1-866-248-3049 or visit our
website at www.simonspeakers.com.

Interior design by Julia Jacintho
Interior illustrations by Priscilla Yuen

Manufactured in the
United States of America

10 9 8 7 6 5 4 3 2 1

Library of Congress Cataloging-in-
Publication Data has been applied for.

ISBN 978-1-5072-1385-8
ISBN 978-1-5072-1386-5 (ebook)

Contains material adapted from the
following title published by Adams
Media, an Imprint of
Simon & Schuster, Inc.:
What Would the Buddha Recycle?
by Rosemary Roberts,
copyright © 2009,
ISBN 978-1-60550-117-8.

The paper used in this book is from
responsibly managed forests.

Contents

Introduction

*Find peace through choosing organic rather
than synthetic clothing.*

Achieve inner calm by converting your home to solar energy.

*Be at one with the world through buying from
your local farmers' market.*

More than 2,500 years ago, a child was born in India. His name was Siddhartha Gautama, and he became the Buddha, a figure who would influence millions of people through the centuries. The Buddha taught us to be conscious of the world and the role you play—the direct impact of your thoughts, choices, and actions. Across the centuries, his message still shines: Be one with that world! Today, that means supporting a sustainable environment. The purpose of this book is to offer you a different perspective on how to transform your eco-footprint through education, conscious living, and self-awareness.

The action of mind (thought) and choice (action) based on intention (environmental safety) is Zen—the school of Mahayana Buddhism that originated in China about 1,200 years ago. You are not simply one, but one of the world whose presence, like the ripple of a pebble tossed into a pond, affects the vibration and well-being of everything and everyone around you. The practice of Zen, as it relates to living in a more environmentally friendly way, is to gain a better understanding of your personal ripple—to more consciously acknowledge the way in which your choices and actions contribute to your health, life, and the planet Earth, adding richness to it.

In these pages, you'll find suggestions about:

- Your use of energy resources
- Mindful housecleaning and washing
- Zen eating and drinking habits
- Green personal care
- Ecologically sound transportation
- Vacationing responsibly

With the added tools offered by Zen you can begin to consciously alter the ramifications of your personal global ripple in a very positive way. Because Zen does not rely on formal religious dogma, it can be incorporated into your life regardless of your religious beliefs and traditional practices. Buddha didn't think of himself as a god, but as a human being who found enlightenment and peace by shedding material excess and understanding his connection to the world. This path is open to anyone.

It's true that the thought of reducing your environmental footprint can seem daunting. But you don't have to turn your life upside down. Mindfully caring for the earth and its inhabitants can be done by making small changes and coming to simple realizations about your lifestyle—which is just how Buddha made his way to Nirvana.

PART ONE

The Zen of Sustainability

CHAPTER ONE

Let the Green Spirit of Zen Lead You

Zen teaches us that a ripple begins as a thought and transforms into an action that moves throughout the universe. Many of us never know the full consequences of our actions, but every now and then we have the opportunity to witness a ripple become a wave.

THE EIGHTFOLD PATH

Within the very heart of Zen are eight tools of right that make every task, every decision, and, consequently, every reaction to your actions purposeful. When used to preserve and honor the earth and the world around, above, and below us, these tools embody the essence of sustainability...the Zen way. The pathway of eight is a tool more than a rule—each part of the pathway is a critical step toward enlightenment and well-being for those on Earth and Earth itself.

1. Right View—*Rethinking Your Perception of Green.*

Becoming sustainable has now become a passion of the masses, and, indeed, a necessary way of life if we are to preserve life on Earth itself...including our own. With consciousness comes opportunity, and living an eco-friendly life has never been easier for the individual, a community, or a nation.

2. Right Thought—*Eco-Friendly Is a Choice.*

Can we ignore what we've learned about the environment so far, or ignore further the rapid fire of new information from a focused scientific community? If we choose to do so, what price for our action—or lack of action—will our children, and our children's children, ultimately pay? With right thought, change becomes possible.

3. Right Speech—*Voicing the Spirit of Environmental Awareness.*

Speaking out about the need for conservation and green technologies, as well as praising others for their efforts, is using right speech. Reciting all the excuses as to why recycling is too much of a hassle is a vibrational assault against the earth.

4. Right Action—*First, Do No Harm.*

Given that every action has a cause and effect, it's important to examine what you think and what you know, and then choose actions that first do no harm—actions that support the well-being of human, plant, and animal, as well as the earth.

5. Right Livelihood—*Seeing the Big Picture.*

Livelihood is your expression of life, the spirit from which you draw and expand upon each and every day. Expressing your ecological footprint in ways that benefit and support all aspects of your life (home, work, and play) is right livelihood.

6. Right Effort—*Going Green One Step at a Time.*

Right effort is about doing what you can, when you can, and because you can. When you apply effort to thinking about the changes you can make toward your green transformation (right thinking), then take action to make those changes (right action), that's right effort. Right effort applies to the smallest change equally as it applies to the largest change.

7. Right Mindfulness—*Environmentally Friendly Intention.*

Beginning a green lifestyle doesn't always come naturally. As you begin this important journey, you'll no doubt be halfway to that store around the corner when you realize, "Hey, I could have walked." Good for you. You're mindful of how you could do better and will be more inclined to do better next time.

8. Right Concentration—*How Big Is Your Footprint?*

Commitment to joining the world community and truly doing your part requires effort and planning. It means applying sincere effort to your environmental education, a dedication to change both in the home and workplace, and a compelling honesty about your responsibility as a world participant. Right concentration may result in the degree of that commitment through learning, doing, and teaching, but it begins in the heart and moves through your spirit.

Once you've mastered these eight rules—and it's not a bad idea to meditate on them for a while—you'll be able to see how their precepts are reflected in the rest of this chapter. These rules give you the philosophical structure you need to fully commit to changing your eco-footprint.

LIVING A GLOBAL COMMUNITY LIFE

In the world of Zen, there is no division or degree of separation between you and your mind, body, or spirit, nor between you and your loved ones, friends, and neighbors, or those who are oceans away. Zen is about recognizing the universal connection to all and doing no harm to yourself or others in any way that causes suffering within the universe. This is the challenge that our global community must adopt; one individual, one community, and one nation at a time. As some countries that were less progressive in the past become more affluent and industrialized, the threat to natural resources and concerns about the destruction of the environment grow. Equally, the reality of harm already done by expansive, thriving countries such as the United States must be faced straight up and honestly; harm that prevails in many practices today cannot be overlooked as a continuing threat.

The world can little afford ignoring that what happens in one part of the globe eventually affects other areas of the planet half a world away. Each person, country, and continent is truly interdependent.

World agencies recognize that we must work together toward protecting sensitive biostructures like coral reefs and diverse ocean populations, managing forests with sustainable growth, sustaining air quality the world over, and reducing the damaging effects and usage of fossil fuels and chemicals that are devastating to humans and the environment. The role of the individual in this profound effort, however, is essential.

The World Sangha

Common to the human condition is a feeling of disconnection. It may be a sense of isolation within your home, among your neighbors, or at work. Buddhism addresses this through the sangha—a community of like-minded people committed to a common goal, in this case, sustainability. Such a community is unstructured, but it can join you to other people around the world who understand the importance of protecting our planet. Often Zen sanghas meet together to practice meditation—a key aspect of Zen—but it's also possible for you to spend time on your own meditating about the earth and your connection to it.

Zen is a journey of enlightenment that allows you to experience the whole of your world. There is no destination, just changing landscapes, many of which overlap to other worlds. Likewise, we are not isolated from other countries. Our suffering is their suffering and theirs is ours. The world's journey is also one of Zen—one of acceptance, understanding, and goodwill to ease all suffering.

The world stage is getting smaller and little can happen in one part of the globe that doesn't eventually affect another place half a world away. No one person, no one country, no one continent is truly independent.

In 1997, under the auspices of the United Nations, representatives met in Kyoto, Japan, to discuss global air quality. The result was the Kyoto Protocol, an international framework for managing greenhouse gases and improving air quality. And more recently, a series of positions aimed at limiting climate change and the further development of global warming was adopted at the 2015 UN Climate Change Conference in Paris.

ELEMENTS OF ZEN

Earth has three main components, all of which have long been a part of Zen practices: the air we breathe, the land we live on, and the water that nourishes us.

A great place to begin your journey to live in harmony with Earth is with the element that speaks to you the most. Do you feel nourished by sunrises and sunsets, love to swim in a clear mountain lake, or delight in a gentle breeze blowing through your hair? Perhaps your idea of a great getaway is up in the mountains, camping among the majestic trees and the scent of pine, or just feeling grounded after a quiet walk on a nearby trail.

Zen involves deep contemplation and is often easier when you begin with an element most "home" to you. If land is your grounding point, why not begin outside in and around your yard? If water nourishes your soul, begin with a water filtration system for your family's drinking source, or by eliminating the chemicals that flow from your drains to the rivers, streams, and the ocean. Commit to reducing your carbon footprint on the air around you by carpooling, walking, or biking when possible.

The Air

Air is one of the main elements in Buddhism (the others are earth, water, and fire). Buddhism associates air with the idea of expansion. For instance, we breathe in air to live, expanding our lungs but then we push it out when we exhale. The air is mostly invisible, but it's by no means empty; it contains millions upon millions of particles, some of which can harm us if we allow the air to be polluted. We travel through the world of air, drawing sustenance from it. For this reason, the care and protection of the air we and all living creatures breathe is of central importance to a Zen approach to the world.

The Land

Land—the earth—sustains life both on the surface and below ground. Soil controls the flow of water over land, filters chemicals, and stores nutrients. It supports the structures that people live and work in. When the soil is neglected, the life that depends on it is damaged as well.

Soil is the outermost layer of the planet. In a way, it functions as the planet's skin, a protective layer. It's made from rocks, plants, and animals that have decayed over hundreds of years—just one inch of topsoil takes up to five hundred years to form. Beneath the surface, a complex ecosystem comprises minerals, water, air, fungi, bacteria, and plant material all working together.

Land is a key element of Zen thought. It's possible to draw sustainable energy from both it and from the plants and animals that live on it. Producing such energy is referred to as biomass. One common method is burning plant material to heat water and generate electricity. Feedstock for biomass power facilities generally includes agricultural waste left over from harvesting, energy crops grown specifically for use as biomass, forestry remains after timber harvesting, and wood left over from mill operations. To provide the most sustainable alternatives, it's best to use plant material waste that is close to the biomass plant to avoid transportation impacts.

Awakening to Geothermal Power

Sustainable energy isn't just available from above ground. It can be found below ground as well. For every 100 meters you go below ground, the temperature of the rock increases about 3°C (37.4°F). Deep under the surface, water sometimes makes its way close to the hot rock and turns into boiling hot water or steam. Wells, some shallow and some miles deep, are drilled into these reservoirs to bring hot water or steam to the surface. These are used to generate electricity and are cleanly released back into nature as either cold water or water vapor. Geothermal energy is most abundant and more easily accessible in places like Hawaii and Alaska where the geothermal reservoirs are closer to the surface. The shifting and moving tectonic plates in these areas enable the water heated from the magma below to escape more easily to the surface. Geothermal electricity is available virtually anywhere but is located much deeper, making retrieval less cost-effective.

The Water

Most of our planet—most of *you*—is made up of water. It's essential for life. The world's oceans are home to some of the largest, smallest, and most diverse animal populations on the planet. The oceans are majestic environments that hold unknown mysteries that humans are only beginning to discover.

Protecting resources like drinking water is paramount for society, but protection often comes only after shortages are permanent or supplies are tainted. All over the world, water wars are frequent as rising populations strain limited supplies.

Water sources like rivers, streams, and aquifers have been tapped for irrigation. But it's possible to make this process more efficient. Water flushed from household toilets and drained from residential washing machines can be converted to graywater with minimal treatment and reused for irrigation. Individual graywater systems are being approved for residences. Not only does graywater offset the demand for treating water to the highest potable standard; it also may actually be beneficial to plants as it's likely to contain nitrogen and phosphorus.

The Flow of Hydropower

Hydropower plants harness the kinetic energy of flowing water to power machinery or make electricity. The most common hydro power begins with a dam that stores the water in a reservoir. Water flowing through the dam spins a turbine, which uses a generator to make electricity and sends it out to the grid.

Because water is not destroyed in the process of creating energy, it is considered a renewable resource. It doesn't produce pollutants as fossil fuels do, and the dams are often used for flood control. Unfortunately, because hydropower relies on the natural water cycle, energy production can be impacted during dry seasons or times of drought. Hydroelectric plants also interfere with the natural flow of rivers and everything that moves along with them, including spawning fish and natural river and tributary flows. Another consideration with dams is thermal pollution, because the water released on the other side of the turbine is often warmer than the water entering. This can have a negative effect on aquatic life that is suited to narrow temperature ranges.

CLIMATE CHANGE

It's practically impossible to listen to the radio, watch TV, or read the news without hearing about global climate change. The majority of scientists agree that action needs to be taken now to stop, and eventually reverse, the trend of global warming. Economists debate the cost of solutions versus the financial benefits of adaptation to new climate conditions rather than discussing the real dangers of not moving forward with a viable plan.

While such problems may seem beyond the effort of an individual, remember that Zen teaches us we are all connected through the planet. Even small actions on your part can have a cumulative effect that goes well beyond you.

A Zen approach to environmental issues views them on a global scale, not merely as local manifestations. While fighting against pollution on a local scale is important, Zen allows you to see this in the context of the entire planet. This is especially important for issues like climate change and the effects of greenhouse gases.

FIRST, DO NO HARM

The Buddha believed that we should avoid harming other lives whenever possible. Certainly it's impossible to go through your life without harming other beings, but Zen cautions that we should be mindful of it, as well as all our actions. Around the globe, the human population affects all forms of life: trees, seagrass, animals, and people. Often the damage we do is the result of beneficial activities performed irresponsibly.

Degradation of natural resources often has a chain effect. For example, consider the impact that clearing acres of rain forest for farming has on both local and global environments. Soil cannot support crops that are harvested on a yearly basis and its productivity quickly diminishes. As income decreases along with the crop yield, farmers abandon the land in search of more fertile fields, increasing pressure on local resources. The deforested land does not absorb rainwater as before, so rainfall causes more water to flow into nearby rivers all at once, flooding downstream villages and cities. However, drought is also an outcome of deforestation.

Part of the reason rain forests are so wet is that trees play a vital role in supplying water to the atmosphere through transpiration; without trees, the water to produce rain simply isn't there. Haphazard deforestation results in patches of remaining forest separated by cleared land. Plants and animals are effectively marooned, isolated from their species. Fewer options can result in inbreeding, weakening the gene pool. Larger species, usually predators, are especially vulnerable to population loss simply because there are so few of them. A bad breeding year, a natural disaster, or a disease can wipe them out. On a global scale, deforestation contributes to a buildup of greenhouse gases; fewer trees mean more carbon dioxide is left in the atmosphere.

Only through education can people gain a better understanding of our interconnectedness to the planet and all it supports. Zen, because it considers humans in relationship to both the environment and to each other, can be a vital part of that education.

Sustainable Energy: Solar and Wind

The sun and wind both have importance in Zen thought. The sun, for instance, is a symbol of enlightenment, of the sort that the Buddha achieved through his meditations. The deva Surya is a deity who embodies the sun.

The wind in Zen is a subject often at the center of meditation. According to some stories, two monks were meditating on a flapping flag. "It is the flag that is moving," said one. "It is the wind that is moving," replied the other. A master, overhearing them, said, "Not the wind, not the flag. *Mind* is moving."

Solar Sutra

Large solar plants, called concentrated solar power (CSP) plants, can accommodate the needs of a small community or can generate enough electricity to flow into the grid and supplement power generated by other means.

Solar power continues to be slightly more expensive than traditional fossil fuel options, but the cost is expected to decrease as more private and public utility plants appear and solar cell technology advances. Proposed government credits and development incentives are playing an enormous role in advancing the research and use of solar.

The Answer Is in the Wind

The practice of Zen involves stillness; a quieting of the mind so that you can tune into the world around you. Often, you'll hear the breeze outside. Perhaps it has a message of global proportions. Throughout history, windmills have been used primarily as grinding mills, sawmills, or even water-pumping mills. Today they are used to harness the wind's kinetic energy. Wind moves the mill's blades, which rotate a shaft that in turn moves gears connected to a generator. The generator creates electricity.

Not only is wind renewable; it's clean and doesn't produce the deleterious by-products that other forms of energy do. Wind energy doesn't depend on process water as do coal and nuclear power. Wind power is generated domestically; there is no dependence on other countries to produce energy for local use. Also, harnessing wind power doesn't require mining operations as coal does, an wind power brings clean, high-tech jobs to farmlands and possibly coastal communities as well. Wind is the fastest-growing energy source, and per kilowatt it is close to the cost of generating electricity using fossil fuels.

The cost of installing windmills is recouped more quickly than other emerging technologies. However, wind turbines require an extensive amount of land, which can make them more difficult to place in urban areas. Besides land availability, wind turbine sites must be located within high wind energy areas either on land or over the water.

Noble Truths about Nuclear Power

The debate about adding more nuclear power in our future plans is enough to make some go...well, nuclear! The concerns are centered on two items: the safe storage of nuclear waste and safety. In a world of terrorist threats, security concerns ratchet up the risk factors.

Concerns are fueled by history: the partial meltdown of a reactor at Three Mile Island near Middletown, Pennsylvania, in 1979, and the explosion and widespread radioactive contamination experienced at the Chernobyl nuclear power plant in the former Soviet Union in 1986.

Sixty nuclear power plants are currently operating in the United States. Waste produced from nuclear power plants includes high-level and low-level radioactive waste. High-level waste is the spent fuel. Although it's depleted, it continues to be radioactive for tens of thousands of years or longer and must be handled using remote-control equipment. The spent fuel is stored temporarily in water-cooled pools and dry casks at nuclear power plants. Permanent storage requires burial of the material deep underground, and there are currently no permanent storage facilities in the United States.

PART TWO

Using Zen to Go Green

CHAPTER TWO

Owning the Shoes
You Walk In

Enlightenment is not a smooth process. Be prepared to stumble, while also appreciating the lessons learned by trial and error. Enlightenment also comes with enjoyment of the process, finding the simple pleasures in learning a new way and being inspired by new goals. Buddha teaches that where you are in the present is exactly where you're supposed to be, so don't waste time on guilt, doubt, or worry— they're worthless. Simply own your shoes and walk forward.

Zen teaches us about personal responsibility: how to honestly evaluate our personal responsibility in creating the world around us, and how to better ourselves through the betterment of others. In terms of a green lifestyle, Zen implores us to take responsibility for our lifestyles and work toward a more peaceful and harmonious relationship with the planet. Maintaining an Earth-friendly home is usually a combination of conserving energy and being conscientious about the products you use and the packaging they come in. Repurposing items not only saves space in the landfills—it also saves money. It's interesting that organic spinach and other mixed greens are now sold in rectangular plastic containers about the size of a shoebox; something about that type of packaging with the label "organic" just seems off target. Nonetheless, it's out there. Rather than feeling too guilty about the packaging, consider repurposing the container for your shoes. They stack nicely and keep the dust off those sexy party shoes worn only a few times a year, while also allowing you to see clearly what shoes are inside.

You can find (or make at home) alternative products to help reduce or eliminate the use of chemicals in cleaning supplies and pest control. Inexpensive products are available that help conserve energy and water while reducing waste. All of these options conspire to save natural resources. An additional benefit to conservation is that it usually saves you money too. This chapter gives you a rundown on how to take care of your house while saving the planet and a couple of bucks at the same time!

CLEANING WITH AWARENESS

Armed with bottles of cleaning solution and various gadgets to help you remove every last speck of dirt, the battle for clean begins. But don't think you have to sacrifice a clean house to be more environmentally friendly. Clean and green aren't mutually exclusive. When you're shopping for environmentally friendly cleaning products, look for a green label and choose natural products that list all their ingredients. Green cleaning products should not contain ingredients such as chlorine, petroleum-based solvents, nonylphenol surfactants, glycol ethers, or dyes. They should be biodegradable and nontoxic. Truly green cleaners are not animal tested—a practice that we should all fiercely oppose.

When evaluating cleaners, choose one that is safe for everyone in the family, safe for the environment, conserves natural resources, and ultimately gets the job done. Avoid unnecessary dyes and fragrances and stay away from extra packaging. Be careful with concentrates. Using a cleanser that comes in concentrated form does save on packaging by allowing consumers to dilute it at home, but take care to avoid exposing people and the environment to the highly concentrated ingredients.

The Simple Path

Baking soda is a wonderful thing and found in just about every kitchen. It's sodium bicarbonate, a naturally occurring compound that is nontoxic and deodorizing. It's also gently abrasive—safe for chrome or enamel. You can mix $1/4$ cup of baking soda with one quart of warm water to make a cleaning solution. Or you can just shake it directly on what you're cleaning. Did I mention it's less expensive, and also typically comes packaged in an environmentally friendly manner?

Here's a list of other natural and less toxic cleaning ingredients and their uses.

- Mix $\frac{1}{2}$ cup of vinegar with 1 gallon of water to clean floors. (Be sure your floor won't be affected by the pH shift. Some materials like marble and no-wax floors are vulnerable to color change and etchings. The manufacturer will be able to tell you if vinegar is safe for your floor.)
- Two parts borax mixed with one part lemon juice can be used to clean the toilet. This is especially effective for removing stains. Spray with vinegar to make sure your cleaning solution will remove microbes.
- A mixture of equal amounts of lemon juice and olive oil is great for polishing unvarnished furniture. For varnished furniture, use $\frac{1}{2}$ cup of warm water and a few drops of lemon juice.
- Use $\frac{1}{4}$ cup of rubbing alcohol mixed with $\frac{1}{2}$ cup of vinegar and 2 cups of water to clean windows. Use newspaper instead of paper towels to wipe windows.
- Sprinkle baking soda on your stainless steel, iron, or copper pots and scrub to clean. (Don't use baking soda on aluminum pots.)

The Peaceful Warrior and Pest Control

Gentle methods of reducing pests and insects in the house are also green methods, and the first step is to remove whatever attracts them. Keep counters and floors clean of food scraps. Avoid dripping faucets and soaking dishes, which serve as a water source enticing insects into the kitchen. Foods that pests find attractive like flour, pasta, and cornmeal can be kept in the refrigerator or in airtight containers.

There are also some natural remedies to control pests in the house. Here is a list of natural ways to rid your home of some of the more common pests without using pesticides.

- Follow a trail of ants to find where they are coming in. Sprinkle chili pepper, dried peppermint, or borax to steer them away.
- For cockroaches, mix borax, sugar, and flour, and sprinkle it in the infested area, or add water and form the mixture into little balls and leave them for the roaches to eat. Also try sprinkling borax behind light switches, under sinks, and in the back of cabinets to kill roaches.
- Feeding a dog or cat brewer's yeast mixed in with their food deters fleas.
- Use cedar chips to drive off moths.
- Buy humane traps that allow you to catch and release vermin.
- Pantries can be kept free of moths and other insects with insect traps that use nontoxic adhesives and attractants.
- Diligent vacuuming can eliminate dust mites. If dust mites are in bedding, wash it regularly and cover pillows and mattresses

in mite-free mattress cases and pillowcases. Another benefit of eliminating pesticides is that you will be able to avoid keeping poisons in your home and the possibility of accidental exposure.

WISE DISHWASHING

The news on dishwashing isn't all bad! Dishwashers are, in most cases, more efficient today than the old sink and tub routine. Researchers at the University of Bonn in Germany determined that using a dishwasher not only cleaned the dishes better—it also saved energy and time. Now you can sit back after dinner and relax, guilt-free. If you do not have a dishwasher, the folks in Bonn have recommendations for getting the most out of handwashing your dishes:

- Don't rinse any of the dishes before washing. This is also true if you are using an automatic dishwasher.
- Use two sinks—one with hot soapy water to wash and one filled with cooler water to rinse.
- Do not go overboard with the soap or detergent. Use only what's needed; it will conserve cleanser and won't over-sud the rinse water.

Phosphorus, an ingredient in many dish detergents, works its way through a wastewater treatment plant, ending up in surface waters and other effluent disposal locations. Many states have already banned high phosphorus detergents, such as Finish and Cascade in their liquid form, from store shelves. Cascade, in the new, easy tablet form does contain phosphorus, but less overall per wash and, therefore, is not part of the ban in some cases. In general, check labels for low phosphorus and chlorine levels before you buy any detergent, and consider switching over to mindful, Earth-friendly products like Method Dish Cubes, Seventh Generation Liquid Dish Detergent, or Biokleen Automatic Dish Powder. Many consumers even swear by homemade dishwashing detergent made by combining equal parts baking soda and borax (found at most supermarkets). Use vinegar as a natural spot-remover in your rinse cycle.

If you are in the market for a new dishwasher, check for Energy Star labels to ensure the model you purchase uses energy efficiently.

COMPASSIONATE CLOTHING CARE

There are a few ways to reduce the impact on the environment when doing the laundry. Washing clothes in cold water saves energy and reduces fading. Using the smallest amount of soap or detergent will also help save money and natural resources. The following tips will show you how.

A Cleansing Journey

What's the difference between soap and detergent? Both soap and detergent use surfactants, which is why they both get stains out. The difference is the source of the surfactants. Soaps tend to be organically based, derived from plant or nut oils, and are generally referred to as oleochemicals. Detergents are synthetic and are usually made from petrochemicals.

Until recently, fossil fuel was relatively inexpensive and easily available, making the synthetics popular ingredients in detergents. However, with fluctuations in the market and concerns about the environmental aspects of obtaining and processing fossil fuels, manufacturers are looking to other surfactant ingredients.

A Disciplined Approach to Stains

For starters, stains are not created equal and some can be a challenge. Organic or protein stains include blood, sweat, and coffee and can be removed using hydrogen peroxide. Fat or oil stains like salad dressing may come out by dousing and rubbing them with cornstarch. Fruit stains like juice or wine are apt to disappear when drenched in boiling water. Make sure to treat the stain as soon as possible.

Earthful Drying

There's no denying that using the heat from the sun to dry clothes saves energy, but clotheslines are rare these days. So if you aren't ready to quit using your dryer cold turkey, you may just want to cut back a little. When you do use your dryer, you can take steps to make it more efficient. Don't overdry clothes. Take out the clothes when they are dry. Don't overload the dryer, and dry similar items together.

Dryer sheets release chemicals as they bounce around in the dryer, making clothes soft and reducing static electricity. They routinely contain chemicals such as chloroform and benzyl acetate that can be harmful to the environment and irritate people's skin. There are also chemical-free products available that treat static electricity and soften clothes and can be used over and over again. Dryer balls have little nubs that help fluff clothes and reduce the static, and can be used again and again. People who suffer from sensitivity to the chemicals used in traditional dryer sheets will find items like dryer balls a great alternative. National Allergy (www.natlallergy.com) carries a variety of products for people with sensitivities and allergies, including AllerTech Reusable Dryer Sheets.

Many of today's new washing machines use more powerful spin cycles without harming clothes. Better spins mean that your clothes require less time tossing around in the dryer because they go in with less surface water still attached. The result is less water used to wash and less gas or electricity for drying.

Some models, for example, no longer offer light, medium, or full load settings because the washer figures it out for you. Once you select the temperature and soil level (light, normal, or heavy), the washer begins to toss the contents, adding a little water each time and then determines the load size based on weight. It only uses the amount of water necessary to achieve a constant saturation.

Higher priced sets with all the bells and whistles, however, aren't always better, so do your homework. Going green doesn't mean wasting your green. Yes, respect for the real value of money is very Zen.

CLEANER AIR LEADS TO HEALING BREATH

Everyone wants to breathe easily, especially when meditating at home. There are a variety of contaminants that can decrease air quality, many of which can be reduced by eliminating the source. Anything from smoking to buying new furniture can help contaminants find their way into your airspace.

The following common types of indoor air pollution can be found in most homes:

- Asbestos is made up of small carcinogenic particles that can lodge in the lungs. The particles enter the air through deteriorating ceiling and floor tiles, or acoustic and fireproofing materials.
- Biological pollutants include mold, mildew, and pet dander. They can cause allergic reactions and aggravate asthma.
- Carbon monoxide is an odorless gas that is produced during incomplete combustion of carbon and can be lethal. Sources include car emissions, fireplaces, and gas stoves.
- Pressed-wood products can emit formaldehyde that can cause headaches and induce asthma.
- Cleaning, maintenance, and hobby products can contain volatile organic compounds that can cause headaches and also pose a long-term cancer risk.
- Lead exposure is generally caused by lead-based paint or contaminated soil. If you are involved in an activity that may produce lead dust, be sure to use lead-safe work practices, which include keeping children out of the area.

- Nitrogen dioxide is produced by unvented kerosene heaters and tobacco smoke.
- Pesticides generally include semi-volatile organic compounds. Being around pesticides for a long time can irritate the respiratory system and cause damage to the liver and central nervous system.
- Radon comes from naturally decaying uranium in soil and water and is the second-leading cause of lung cancer. The US surgeon general has encouraged everyone to have their homes tested for radon.
- Fireplaces and wood-burning stoves can produce particles. When burning, try to ventilate the area to avoid irritation to eyes and respiratory systems.

Bathroom and kitchen fans can be used to exhaust air directly to the outside and improve the ventilation rate. However, if left open, ventilation fans exchange a considerable amount of air, which waste energy by requiring extra heating or cooling.

If you're getting rid of household products that are labeled poison, danger, warning, or caution, don't throw them in the trash or pour them out. Find out about household hazardous waste collection centers or pickup service in your local area.

CHAPTER THREE

Mindful Dining

Enjoying each meal, no matter how big or small, and taking time to be grateful for what you prepare for those you love, is Zen. Nourishment—vital to maintaining health—is a means of honoring the body. Precooked packaged foods containing additives are an insult to the body, as poisons, whose harmful effects may not be seen immediately, contaminate the body's energy and block its ability to function at its best.

Imagine, for a moment, the delight of eating an organic orange, taking in the first zest of chemical free fragrance as you begin to peel the skin, and then tasting the dance of citrus flavors on your tongue. Imagine too the beneficial vitamin C and other aspects of the fruit, all in harmony with your body, nurturing and naturally healing.

Now imagine nuking a prepackaged meal. Do you feel soothed as you peel the plastic lid from the container? While the flavor may be appealing, consider the fillers, the sugars, and other additives, such as preservatives (nitrates), being absorbed. Intellectually you know it's harmful, and yet you proceed with your meal. Eating such a meal is to live and eat unconsciously, thus bringing harm to your body. Zen allows you the opportunity to consider the choices you make and, one meal at a time, choose differently.

Where organic food was once limited to specialty stores and markets, making cost a limiting factor for many families on a budget, it's now available almost everywhere including on the Internet! Organic food has even become an important part of restaurants, and food services are being revamped in school cafeterias and corporate lunch counters. This chapter delves into what organic really means, the benefits of going organic, and the many options for bringing organic food to the table.

THE ORIGINS OF ORGANIC

The definition of *organic* varies depending on who is involved in the conversation. Conventional wisdom is that the term *organic* refers to the growing, raising, or processing of food without drugs, synthetic chemicals, or hormones using methods that conserve natural resources and limit the effects on the environment. But how do you know if something is truly organic?

Foods meeting the USDA, UK, and Canadian requirements for being organic will have a USDA seal. To obtain the seal, foods must be 95 percent organic. Foods using only organic products and methods may also state "100% organic" on the packaging. A lower level of organic certification is available for foods that are 70 to 95 percent organic. These foods can be labeled as "made with organic ingredients." Organic foods should not be confused with natural or whole foods, however. Foods labeled natural and whole are not held to the same healthy standards as organic.

HOMEGROWN NOURISHMENT

If you want to literally put your own fruits and veggies on the table, starting an organic garden or farm might be an option. When it comes to organic farming or gardening, local groups and county agriculture agencies can be exceptionally helpful because they are aware of local conditions, what grows well, and what problems you might encounter. Check out cooperatives and extension services associated with nearby universities or county agencies for more information. Regardless of where you live, you can take simple measures to make your garden truly organic:

- Use natural fertilizers like grass cuttings and leaves to enrich the natural soil.
- Add mulch and compost to help the soil retain water. The less you have to water, the more water you'll conserve.

- Buy organic seeds. USDA-certified organic seeds will not have genetic modifications.
- Include plants like cilantro, dill, and fennel to encourage visits from ladybugs and other predatory insects that will help control pests.
- As your garden grows, use organic methods to keep insect pests, mildew, weeds, and fungus at bay.

SPIRITUAL SHOPPING

According to the Organic Trade Association (OTA), the sale of organic foods increased 5.9 percent in 2018 alone, bringing in $48 billion in sales. More and more fresh, whole food, and organic grocery stores are popping up across the United States, and traditional grocers and food producers are taking notice.

The Novelty Becomes the Norm

Some of the fastest growing food chains today are, in fact, those that offer a greater variety of whole foods. Consumers must still be their own advocates and read the labels, as most stores continue to blend in traditional items with the healthier choices.

Feeling pressure from growing specialty organic stores, more mainstream grocery stores are including a variety of organic food in their inventories as well. Many stores have even started their own lines of organic foods.

Giving Back to the Community

Smaller independent markets consistently buy locally grown fruits and vegetables that are fresh and seasonal. That means the produce people eat spends more time ripening on the vine than traveling across the country—or the world. A growing movement encourages food labels to include information about how many miles the product traveled from the farm to the store. This information would allow shoppers to purchase more locally grown produce and avoid food that's made a longer haul.

Farmers' Markets and Health Food Stores

There are also more specialized farmers' markets and health food stores where people can purchase lines of organic and natural foods that might not be available elsewhere. The term *farmers' market* can mean anything from an open-air market where farmers and their families sell directly to consumers, to full-scale stores utilizing distribution networks to bring a combination of locally and internationally grown produce to their bins. Many cities support locally grown fruits, vegetables, and plants by providing space for weekend markets. Farmers or their families are often on hand to answer questions and offer explanations.

Health food stores carry fresh produce similar to what you would find at a farmers' market, but they also offer organic, natural, and whole foods. Items sold at health food stores range from baby food to breakfast cereal to soups. Stores may also carry special dietary foods such as gluten-free products. Much like conventional grocery stores, health food stores carry personal items, like shampoo and soap, along with nutritional supplements and homeopathic treatments. Some health food stores have a café offering a selection of healthful sandwiches and snacks.

Edible Gifts from the Earth

If you would like your food to come to you, try community supported agriculture (CSA), which allows you to buy "shares" in a local farm. You will receive a basket of produce every week or month. You can pick up your basket at a prearranged location or it may be delivered to your home or office. Visit www.localharvest.org/csa to find participating farms in your area.

WALKING THE VEGETARIAN PATH

Vegetarianism—a lifestyle based on a choice not to consume meat, fish, or poultry—has been practiced for thousands of years. Being a vegetarian does not automatically exclude dairy products or eggs from the diet; that's an individual choice. Vegans eat no animal flesh or products and abstain from wearing or using animal products such as leather, silk, wool, lanolin, or gelatin. Dietary vegans adhere to a strict diet, but are amenable to using animal products.

The vegetarian movement cites conservation and animal cruelty as reasons to follow their eating lifestyle. Rather than allowing cows and other animals to graze and forage naturally, most are confined and fed grain and corn that is grown using pesticides and transported to farms by truck and rail. Overall, the meat consumes massive amounts of energy, burdening the soil, groundwater, surface water, and air.

THE POWER OF PROTEIN

There was a time when we would pick up a package of chicken breasts on sale and marvel at the size and plumpness of the meat. Today, we know that unless otherwise noted on the packaging, the large size of the individual breasts is most likely a sign that growth hormones have been added to the chicken's diet—a health risk, according to many nutritional experts. Whether fish, chicken, pork, or beef, meat is still a staple of many meals, and consumers need to educate themselves on how the animals are raised, allowing them to choose the meat they buy more conscientiously.

The Tao of Fish

Fish can be a good source of protein without the saturated fats in other meats. Fish also contain essential vitamins and minerals including omega-3 fatty acids, which have been shown to prevent heart disease and may even help brain development. Many fish are caught in the wild; others such as salmon are frequently farm raised.

Sustainable Sourcing

Managing the catching of wild fish can be a complicated process because many fish are caught in international waters. More and more organizations are working toward safer practices for catching fish to ensure that marine populations are maintained and are able to flourish over the coming decades.

The Marine Stewardship Council is a nonprofit organization that works internationally to certify fisheries based on the type of fish caught and the methods used to catch the fish. A variety of large grocery chains, looking to support sustainable fishing, have pledged to improve buying practices. In Alaska, state officials are monitoring the salmon and at any sign of decline will put a halt to fishing. Studies show that unless fishing is curbed or controlled, many populations are not expected to last until the middle of this century. If precautions are not taken, populations of fish such as orange roughy, Chilean sea bass, Pacific rockfish, sharks, and bluefin tuna may never recover.

Overfishing decreases a population to the point where it cannot replenish itself through natural breeding. This has serious repercussions for the entire ecosystem as species are depleted and are unable to fulfill their traditional roles as predator or prey.

Whether purchasing fish or actually catching it yourself, here are a few things to remember:

- Whether in a store or restaurant, ask where the fish came from and how it was caught. Was the salmon raised on a farm or caught wild in Alaska? Farm-raised salmon, which typically contain less healthy omega-3 fatty acids than their wild counterparts, require an inordinate amount of protein to feed on, and farms routinely discharge concentrated waste untreated into the ocean. Alaskan fisheries have been rated environmentally responsible by the Monterey Bay Aquarium Seafood Watch organization.

- Opt for oysters, scallops, squid, and clams over grouper, tuna, and shark. Marine life that's lower on the food chain can reproduce more quickly and replenish populations more easily while larger life forms take longer. However, because these animals are bottom feeders, they can ingest toxins from sediments more easily, making selection of farm-raised versus wild-raised fish more important.

- Don't discard fishing gear in the water. Tangled lines and hooks can hurt or kill unsuspecting marine life such as turtles and seabirds.
- Avoid protected areas, which allow exhausted fish populations to recover. By staying away, you can support replenishment of the species.
- Put down that seashell. It's important that people avoid taking certain seashells from the beach or purchasing them from tourist shops and craft stores. Enclosed, or conch, shells are often homes to sea life that depend on them for protection.

Be Mindful of Mercury

Fish offer many nutritional benefits; however, they also carry chemicals and contamination absorbed from feeding and living in the water. Mercury is one particularly adverse element.

The EPA has issued warnings for certain types of sea life and offers guidelines for the amount of fish and shellfish consumers should eat. Certain people, particularly pregnant women and small children, are advised to stay away from fish with high levels of mercury because it hinders neural development. Shark, swordfish, king mackerel, and tilefish often contain dangerous amounts of mercury. Shrimp, canned light tuna, salmon, pollock, and catfish have lower levels of mercury and are safe to eat in moderation. More information on the advisory can be found at www.epa.gov.

A KARMIC CONUNDRUM

Animals have long been bred for human consumption. The move to organic meat is bringing to light the treatment of farm animals. Many shoppers are choosing to purchase meat that has been raised more humanely, allowed to graze freely, and not fed hormones and antibiotics.

Researchers at Johns Hopkins University studied the use of antibiotics in poultry farming at one of the largest US producers to determine if the practice was economically beneficial. Based on the results, the drugs did help chickens grow larger; however, the money made from larger chickens did not offset the cost of the drugs. Furthermore, health researchers are beginning to question the health effects on humans where added hormones may increase the risk of disease.

Organically raised meat is becoming more commonplace. Many ranchers strive to provide sustainable farming while providing good living conditions for the animals, but there are still concerns about many animals raised as food.

If you are having a hard time finding pasture-raised meat at local grocers, check out http://eatwild.com. This searchable website allows shoppers in the United States to find local pasture-raised meat. Locations are sorted by state along with a summary of the farm and contact information.

UNENLIGHTENED EATING

Products lining supermarket shelves may not be as innocent as they look. With advances in technology, scientists have been able to manipulate the genes of common foods to bring out positive traits. Similarly, some processed foods have additives that might not be obvious.

Genetic modification speeds up the process of development by inserting specific genes into a plant or animal without going through the trial-and-error process of breeding—that is, breeding good qualities with other good qualities to get the best of both and avoid the undesirable traits. An additional use of genetic modification has been to combine traits from different plants to obtain a very different outcome. This method has been used to grow human insulin in corn for use by diabetics.

The FDA approves genetically modified foods individually based on reports submitted by agricultural companies. If the genetically modified food is shown to be as safe as its unmodified counterpart, approval is granted. The Union of Concerned Scientists has asked the FDA to require labeling of genetically altered food; however, unless reports indicate a difference between the altered and unaltered food, no label is required.

As of 2018, in the United States large amounts of the food you eat are genetically modified:

- 95 percent of sugar beets
- 94 percent of soybeans
- 88 percent of feed corn

As well, chances are if you use canola oil or eat corn, papaya, potatoes, or tomatoes, you have tasted genetically modified food. Numerous crops, including corn, cotton, canola, and soybeans, have been genetically altered to be resistant to certain insects.

Objections to the use of genetically modified foods include both environmental and health concerns. It is uncertain whether plants that are genetically modified for pest resistance could harm unintended and desirable insects. There is also concern that target insects could actually become immune to the pesticides. Environmental concerns include the potential for engineered crops to cross-breed with weeds. Altering crops to resist herbicides could result in mighty weeds undeterred by herbicides. Health concerns include the potential for allergens to be introduced as part of the genetic modification, causing dangerous reactions in some people. Overall, many people are concerned with the unknown effects that genetically modified food could have on their health.

Impure Foods, Processed Foods

Processed food is likely to contain food additives, many of which researchers are citing as a health concern, like excessive nitrates. Additives help extend the life of some foods, add nutrition, or change a food's consistency. Some additives are relatively straightforward, and by reading the label you will know what has been added. Some, however, are less conspicuous. This is of particular concern if you have allergies or are trying to avoid certain foods like meat.

Food additives can cause extreme allergic reactions such as anaphylactic shock, which causes breathing problems and loss of consciousness. Also associated with allergies to foods like peanuts, anaphylactic shock can be fatal if it is not treated.

The Dharma of Dining

Mindful consumers are changing the way the restaurant industry operates, from the fats used in cooking to plate size and even energy consumption. Some green restaurants serve only organic or natural food.

Restaurants use energy for cooking food and keeping it refrigerated as well. Dishwashers use a lot of resources, and thermostats are set to keep patrons happy. Many cities and towns work with small businesses, including restaurants, to help reduce their impact on the environment.

The Green Restaurant Association certifies restaurants, coffee shops, and college and university cafeterias that operate in sustainable ways. Information on their certification process can be found at http://dinegreen.com.

Consumers wield power with their wallets. When dining out, ask questions about the food. For example, many of the fish served at restaurants are not recommended for consumption either because of mercury concentrations or overfishing. The server may not know the answers to all the questions, but the management does. For larger chain restaurants, consider contacting members of the board with your concerns about the food they serve. Readers can refer to Chapter 8 for successful ideas on how to get your point across with companies.

The Heart of the Home

Eastern philosophy calls the kitchen the heart of the home because of its tendency to be a gathering place, and a place where love and intention go into every meal as good energy. A settled mind, consciously tossing the ingredients for meatloaf in a bowl, can be more than just a mundane task mixing meat and egg. Through thought and touch, it becomes a means of sending your love for your family into the meal itself—energy delivered from your heart, to your hands, to your family...much more than just a meatloaf.

Conserving traditional energy in your kitchen, however, is a big part of reducing your impact on the planet. Microwaves heat food much more efficiently than standard ovens and stovetops. They don't require preheating, nor do they take as long to cook food. There have been concerns regarding the way microwaves heat, but there has been no proof that they damage food.

There is concern, however, with respect to the temperature of the food. Because microwaves heat unevenly, you can easily burn your mouth. Heating baby bottles in the microwave is not recommended for this reason.

Cooking plastic in the microwave may cause a chemical breakdown of the material and transfer of chemicals to food, which may linger and cause havoc in the body. Only use plastics for their intended method. Take-home Styrofoam should not be used to reheat any leftovers. If you really want to play it safe, do not use plastics in the microwave. Put your food on microwave-safe glass or ceramic dishes instead.

Other ways to conserve energy in the kitchen include using as small an oven as possible. The larger the oven, the more energy it takes to heat to the proper temperature. Don't forget, ovens are made to keep heat inside, so you can turn off the oven before the timer goes off, and your food will continue to cook. Glass and ceramic retain heat better than metal; switching will reduce the temperature as much as 25 degrees. When using the stove, make sure the burner fits the pan; an uncovered burner wastes heat. Always use a lid when heating items on the stove for the same reason.

CHAPTER FOUR

Right Drinking, Right Action

*Zen teaches that the human body is a temple
that should be kept pure. Choosing to drink only nourishing
fluids that keep both your temple and the earth clean and nurtured
shows your awakened wisdom and awareness of right action.*

As with solid foods, how you achieve hydration—through liquid—matters. Good hydration is vital, but fluids containing too much sugar or contamination by chemicals are poison to your body, hampering digestion and altering hormones that your brain and other functions rely upon.

THE PURITY OF WATER

Without it, people have only days to live. It regulates metabolism and controls body temperature. It moves things around, from joints to food through the digestive system. It's calorie-free and available at almost everyone's fingertips. And water is water, right? Not so fast. Some water really is more environmentally friendly than other water.

Bottle or Tap

Water bottles have become fashion accessories, but ongoing controversy over the plastics used for water and other liquids is rising. If you're going to fill up a plastic sports bottle to go, it's best not to leave it in the car or anywhere where heat from the sun can force chemicals to leach into the liquid.

Bottling companies rarely put the source of the water on the bottle. That's because chances are it didn't come from the clear running stream shown on the bottle. The labels do include contact information for the company, so consumers can call to find out the source of their bottled water.

Delivering millions of gallons of water in separate bottles is incredibly inefficient and damaging to the earth, in both processing and transportation. Rather than taking advantage of existing treatment and distribution systems, bottlers individually package their water and ship it across the country. Plastic bottles are made from petroleum, and trucking them across country uses a lot of gas. The surge in bottled water has left mountains of plastic in its wake. Plastic bottles can be recycled for use in a variety of products, from other bottles to carpet, but most inevitably end up in landfills and incinerators all over the country.

According to the Container Recycling Institute, if people recycled 70 percent of the bottles they purchased for one year, greenhouse gases could be reduced by 20,000 metric tons of carbon equivalent. It would also save the equivalent of 600,000 barrels of crude oil needing to be extracted and processed.

In the United States, currently only ten states have bottle bills that require refund systems for returning used water bottles. Companies that purchase recycled bottles for use in manufacturing prefer to buy plastics from states with bottle bills. The recycling streams from these states contain only plastic bottles, making them much easier to use because additional sorting isn't necessary.

There has been quite a bit of debate lately over whether people should reuse single-use water bottles or toss them out. (Single-use bottles are the ones the water comes in from the store, not the sport bottles made to be reused over and over again.) The concern is twofold: whether the bottles can be adequately cleaned to remove bacteria, and whether the actual cleaning promotes the release of chemicals from the plastic. This is in addition to the safety concerns being raised about whether plastic bottles are safe overall.

Disposable bottles have narrow necks which makes washing them nearly impossible. Bacteria from people's hands and mouths make their way into the bottles and can make people sick. The primary concern is the releasing of chemicals called phthalates during any process where heat is present, including bottles sitting in the cup holders of your car. Phthalates are added to some plastic to keep it flexible so it won't crack. Avoid water bottles with the recycle number three in the triangle on the bottom of the bottle. Water bottles with the recycle numbers one and two are considered safe.

Phthalates, the most common being di (2-ethylhexyl) phthalate, are suspected to be endocrine disruptors that interfere with reproductive organs of both males and females.

The FDA has approved phthalates in plastics that are used to produce food and drink containers, but other agencies like the National Institute of Environmental Health Sciences (NIEHS) and the Centers for Disease Control and Prevention (CDC) are concerned with the potential impacts of phthalates in plastic.

Some great guides that explain the common plastics used around the home and their level of safety are http://chemicalsafetyfacts.org and www-tc.pbs.org/strangedays/pdf/StrangeDaysSmartPlasticsGuide.pdf.

SODA OUTFLOW

The move to organics hasn't only affected food; it's made a difference in the beverage industry too. Soda consumption declined somewhat between 2010 and 2018, from 45.5 gallons per capita per year to 38.8 gallons. That's an encouraging trend, but it's still a very high figure.

One 20-ounce soda contains 17 teaspoons of sugar and 250 calories. Just one soda a day will increase a child's potential to contract type 2 diabetes by 60 percent—and don't forget about tooth decay! Drinking soda is like soaking your teeth in a sugar bath.

If you need to have that fizz when it comes to drinks, there are a number of organic and healthy options to choose from. A number of companies make fruit spritzers, carbonated water in flavors like black cherry, mango, and tangerine. They're generally found in the seltzer water aisle at the grocery.

Speaking of which, you can also consider club soda or seltzer water. Seltzer water is filtered water that's been carbonated. Club soda is water that's had minerals and mineral salts added—just be careful to watch the sodium content when minerals have been added.

MILK

Milk is a primary source for calcium and vitamin D. A 1-cup serving—8 ounces—supplies 30 percent of the daily recommended amount of calcium and 25 percent of vitamin D. Milk also contains significant amounts of protein, potassium, vitamin A, vitamin B_{12}, riboflavin, niacin, and phosphorus. Still, controversy over the dairy industry and the safety of milk is growing. Dairy cows in large numbers are quite a burden on the planet. A dairy cow can produce 120 pounds of manure a day, and cows account for 28 percent of global emissions of methane, a greenhouse gas.

Antibiotics and growth hormones are becoming a concern for consumers. Many dairy cows are given bovine growth hormones (BGH) to encourage milk production and antibiotics to ward off infection.

Not only do consumers ingest elevated hormones that our bodies cannot tolerate; we're also getting added antibiotics that we surely don't need. Organic milk has increased in popularity as people become more aware of the antibiotics and hormones given to cows. Consumers would be wise to check milk containers and consider purchasing only those brands (organic or not) that specifically state no hormone or antibiotic is used.

Wise Alternatives

If you are planning to subtract dairy products from your diet, then rice, coconut, or almond milk can be good replacements for cow's milk. While soy has become a popular milklike product, it is not milk and some in the medical community are concerned about studies that show increased soy in the diet may be more harmful than helpful.

Rice, almond, and coconut milks have a mild sweet taste and can be used instead of dairy milk. They work well in baked goods such as breads and muffins and in breakfast foods such as waffles and pancakes. Once criticized by the dairy industry as unhealthy, a great deal is now being learned about the benefits of coconut milk, reversing the trend. Incidents of cancer, diabetes, and digestive disorders are far rarer among residents of the South Pacific—where coconut milk, meat, and oil are staples of the daily diet—than they are in people with traditional Western diets.

You can find a variety of great books on the benefits and use of coconut products in most health food stores. Bruce Fife, author of *The Coconut Oil Miracle*, walks readers through the history behind the confusion of coconut products, and how many people are now using nature's elixir to help build their immune system and to prevent heart disease and a host of other ailments. While most health food stores carry a variety of healthy coconut milk products, natural health experts warn against processed (pasteurized) coconut oil products commonly found in grocery stores, and suggest cold-pressed products for their increased quality and health benefits.

A QUENCHABLE THIRST

It seems you can't turn a corner without running into a coffee shop. Even young kids are well versed in all the coffees available, swaggering up to the counter to order their own café latte or cappuccino. Tea shops are also cropping up, and many watering holes offer both beverages in a variety of flavors.

Coffee: An Awakening

Few things match the aroma of fresh-ground beans brewing in the morning, but it comes with a price to the environment. Often, when land is cleared and coffee trees are planted, pesticides and fertilizers are needed to support an increasing demand. Some organizations combat this by encouraging shade-grown coffee, where trees are either planted within the existing forests or other plants, like fruit trees, are incorporated into the planting. Fewer fertilizers and pesticides are needed with this method. The shade provided by the trees protects the plants from direct sun and rain and helps maintain soil quality. This means fewer weeds, reducing the need for fertilizers and herbicides. The shade also provides homes for birds that feed on insects, eliminating the need for pesticides. When the natural forest is left intact, migratory birds and other native species are impacted less.

"Green" Tea

Tea—real tea—comes from evergreen plants in India, China, Africa, Japan, and Sri Lanka. Its soothing flavor not only calms the soul but is reported to reduce inflammation, improve immunity, and even fight cavities. Organizations such as the USDA and the Organic Trade Association (OTA) encourage environmentally friendly methods of growing tea. Incorporating nature into the growing process can help avoid the need for pesticides, herbicides, and synthetic fertilizers.

Juice and Its Journey

Orange juice can be green. Before gulping down your juice on the way out the door, consider where it came from and how it got to your refrigerator. Pesticides have been used to protect crops, but organic companies are leading the charge toward less pesticide use. Organic fruit juice generally relies on family farms to provide the needed fruits and vegetables.

ALCOHOL'S ORGANIC FLOW

When it comes to the environment, many wineries have, or are working toward, a certified organic designation. For a wine to be labeled "100% organic," the grapes must have been grown in completely organic conditions and sulfites must not have been added. If a wine is made from 95 percent organic ingredients, it can post the organic label and cannot have added sulfites. The organic beer label means that the barley, hops, and other ingredients are grown and processed without pesticides, fungicides, and fertilizers. Organic beer can be purchased at many stores, especially those catering to whole and organic foods.

Many local microbreweries and vintners make organic beers and wines. By buying locally, shoppers are reducing the travel miles associated with getting the drinks from farm to market. For those feeling particularly bold, home brewing and winemaking is also an option. Organic ingredients can be purchased at the local farmers' market or grocery store. If you are interested in learning more about home brewing, check out www.homebrewersassociation.org.

CHAPTER FIVE

Awakening to Green Personal Care

A life of Zen is a life where personal care is self-care and self-love.
It is to honor one's self through faith, virtue and deeds, wisdom,
and gratitude. Some confuse the shedding of desire to mean
denying themselves of goods of quality. Nothing could be further
from Buddha's way. It's only when the price of a product is the basis
of a purely envious purchase rather than the quality of a product
that one would be in conflict with the practice of Zen.

The variety of natural personal care merchandise—from makeup to bath products—has grown, giving conscientious consumers more products to choose from at affordable prices. From natural to organic, there is a lot to consider when selecting products. Try to avoid excess product packaging. It is possible to choose products that aren't harmful to the environment and still bring out your natural beauty. This chapter gives information on skin- and haircare products, and it identifies what the green issues are and how to choose them.

SHOW YOUR SKIN LOVING-KINDNESS

Your skin is your largest organ, absorbing more, and faster, than any other access point. Consider the lotion you typically use; the endless list of compounds and chemicals found on the label are quickly absorbed through your skin directly into the bloodstream. The Environmental Working Group (EWG) is a watchdog agency comprised of scientists, engineers, and policy experts who sift through scientific data in search of potential risks to people and the environment. The group works in a variety of different consumer and environmental protection areas, including the beauty industry. The EWG maintains Skin Deep, a guide on the chemical ingredients of thousands of personal care products.

The Skin Deep guide can be found online at www.ewg.org. Here is a list of ten things you can do when it comes to choosing safer personal care alternatives:

1. Read the fine print on labels.
2. When it comes to soap, go mild. Strong soaps can remove natural moisturizers.

3. Cut back on fragrance to avoid allergic reactions.

4. Don't go for dark hair dyes. They may contain coal tar ingredients.

5. Avoid baby powder. It's not healthy for babies to breathe it.

6. Avoid giving children under six fluoridated toothpaste.

7. Avoid nail polish to avoid exposure to toluene and acetone. Otherwise, make sure you use polish in a well-ventilated area.

8. Lighten up your use of cologne. Many fragrances contain phthalates (endocrine disruptors) and parabens (chemicals linked to breast cancer).

9. Try to cut back on the number of products used.

10. Use the lists in EWG's Skin Deep guide to find personal care products with minimal amounts of chemicals.

TESTING ON SENTIENT BEINGS

When looking for cruelty-free cosmetics, look for the leaping bunny logo. The leaping bunny logo is awarded by the Coalition for Consumer Information on Cosmetics, an organization made up of eight national animal rights groups. The coalition works with companies to promote nonanimal testing and is making progress in the United States and around the world. Their shopping guides are available online at www.leapingbunny.org and through their Cruelty-Free app to help you find cruelty-free products.

Although efforts have been made to reduce and eliminate animal testing, it is still the primary method of providing data on most cosmetics. Cosmetic testing is usually performed on rabbits, rats, mice, guinea pigs, and dogs—a vile practice. Advances in technology have allowed companies to use computer models, in vitro testing, and other methods to test products, but animal testing continues to be a contentious topic.

Authentic Packaging

Efficient packaging promotes a healthy environment by ensuring everything remains safe during shipping and nothing is wasted. You can look for products that use recycled content in their packaging, and you can also recycle some packaging material.

Holistic Skin Care

Products that are used in natural skin care usually include botanical extracts and essential oils, but that doesn't mean all the ingredients are natural. The USDA certifies organic food, but not personal care items. That gives companies some leeway when it comes to labeling, making it difficult for consumers to know whether a product is natural or organic.

Following is a list of some organic skin care lines that contain organic ingredients:

- Dr. Hauschka Skin Care (www.dr.hauschka.com/en_US/) offers customers a holistic approach to skin care that relies on plant extracts to bring out a person's essential beauty. If you don't know what products are best for your skin type, you can answer a series of questions on the website and be directed to a line of skincare products, or, if you need personal service, an aesthetician will answer your questions.

- Juice Beauty (www.juicebeauty.com) carries a line of cleansers, toners, exfoliants, and moisturizers made from freshly squeezed organic juices. The company uses USDA-certified organic growers for the juice, honey, and aloe vera in their skincare products. Because the USDA doesn't certify personal care products, Juice Beauty designs their own organic labels indicating their discrete purchasing practices.

- Kiss My Face (www.kissmyface.com) was started in an old New York farmhouse by a vegetarian duo back in the 1980s. The company now carries a line of 150 all-natural products that have eliminated the use of unnecessary chemicals. The company believes personal care need not be sacrificed when it comes to protecting the environment.

- Nature's Gate (http://naturesgate.com) develops personal care products using natural botanicals so that their products are environmentally friendly. Not only that—the company also sells all its products in recycled packaging.

HEALING HAIR CARE

Many companies that produce organic skin care products also carry haircare products. A benefit of organic shampoos and haircare products is the absence of synthetic surfactants. These chemicals can persist through wastewater treatment plants and septic systems to end up in ground and surface water.

Here are a few companies that sell lines of environmentally friendly haircare products:

- Terressentials (www.terressentials.com) was selected as a top product in 2004 by *The Green Guide* magazine. Their products are 100 percent natural and chemical-free. There are no detergents or synthetic fragrances in these shampoos.
- Aubrey Organics (www.aubreyorganics.com) was started more than fifty years ago when Aubrey Hampton developed his natural haircare product line. After finding success in Manhattan salons, he expanded the line. Aubrey Organics also includes hair spray and other styling products to help perfect a manageable do.
- California Baby (www.californiababy.com) offers a selection of natural and organic hair care and other products for babies, kids, and adults with sensitive skin. Jessica Iclisoy, who was concerned about putting chemicals on her baby boy's noggin, started the business.

Moral Makeup

Like haircare and other organic products, makeup may cost a little more than at a conventional store, but the costs are comparable to other specialty lines. Some natural or organic makeup might be found in health food stores or whole food grocers, but a larger variety is available online. Many of the natural makeup lines rely on powder foundations as opposed to liquid to avoid ingredients that are more likely to cause irritation. Here's a sampling of websites that carry organic and natural makeup that are cruelty free:

- bareMinerals (www.bareminerals.com) has become a trusted natural source of makeup products. Tip: If there's a bareMinerals store near you, it's worth visiting and having a consultant confirm the shades that are best for your skin type. Armed with the right information, you can easily order from the Internet or buy as you go with confidence. The extra few tips you'll pick up from the consultant are great for application as well. It's not rocket science, but a little instruction can go a long way.

- Burt's Bees (www.burtsbees.com) is a name that's common at retail counters with lip balm and hand creams, but the company also produces makeup. The company was started by two friends looking for a good use for one of the friend's (Burt's) beeswax. The company now makes a variety of Earth-friendly products. Better yet, the packaging is Earth friendly as well.

- Canarias Cosmetics (http://canariascosmetics.com) carries a variety of makeup designed for sensitive skin. Ingredients include mica, zinc oxide, titanium dioxide, and refined iron oxides.

As with other skin-sensitive recipes, Canarias products don't include any oils, fragrances, or preservatives.

Specialty shops also carry lines of organic and natural makeup. Check your favorite brand to see whether it carries a line of organic and natural products.

IMPURE AEROSOLS

Much of the concern about using aerosols in products like deodorants and hairsprays comes from the use of chlorofluorocarbons, or CFCs. First developed in the late 1920s, CFCs became widely used as coolants for refrigerators and air conditioners, cleaning agents for electronics, and propellants for aerosols. In the 1970s, scientists discovered that CFCs were eating away at the ozone layer, damaging its ability to protect Earth from the sun's harmful rays. CFCs also trap heat in the atmosphere and contribute to global warming. Because of these concerns, the EPA banned the use of CFCs in aerosols in 1978. CFCs are being phased out under the Montreal Protocol, administered by the United Nations Environment Programme (UNEP). As part of the agreement, industrialized nations were required to stop using CFCs by January 1, 1996, with developing nations following suit by the year 2010. Today, 197 nations abide by the Montreal Protocol.

Aerosols should be used in well-ventilated areas to avoid health risks. Aerosol cans are made of steel that can be recycled. They must be emptied before they are placed in the recycle bin to avoid explosion.

FOR THE DIVINE FEMININE

Once a month, women of childbearing age menstruate, necessitating the use of boxes and boxes of tampons and sanitary napkins. Disposable tampons that are flushed down the toilet are removed from the wastewater as they enter the bar screen. There, tampons and other larger items are removed and taken to a landfill for disposal. Sanitary napkins thrown in the trash are either taken to a landfill or incinerated. Either way, feminine hygiene products create waste.

If your green living takes you on an outdoor adventure, you may not have the option of scheduling it around your menstrual cycle. There is no conclusive evidence that menstruating women are more likely to be attacked by a bear or shark. To be on the safe side, park rangers recommend that, when hiking, women wear tampons and double-bag their waste.

If you are particularly concerned with the waste produced and are willing to add to your laundry load, consider trying reusable sanitary pads. A variety of pads on the market have other benefits besides reducing waste. The reusable pads are made from 100 percent cotton and do not include irritating fragrances, deodorants, or other chemicals. They come in a variety of sizes and, over time, can save money when compared to single-use tampons and pads. Other options include the Keeper, made from latex, and the Moon Cup, made from silicone; these menstrual cups can hold up to 1 ounce of flow for up to twelve hours. If you are interested, check out these and other reusable menstrual options at sites like https://periodaisle.com.

CHAPTER SIX

Conscious Clothing

In Buddhism, karma is recognized as the cause and effect of the universe. If something good—or green—is done, the results are positive and healthy. In the world of Zen, waste and disruption are equated with bad karma, which is harmful to Earth and her inhabitants. Avoiding synthetic fibers and repurposing old clothes will always bring good karma!

True enlightenment can only come when you are fully aware and conscious of your responsibility to yourself and to Earth. More and more options are now available for choosing sustainable clothing that is environmentally responsible. Today's designs incorporate bright bold colors with professional and trendy styles that blend in with the other garments strutting down the catwalk.

Clothing starts with either renewable or nonrenewable feedstock, which is treated and woven, dyed, and sewn to produce a piece of clothing. The clothing may have started out as a fossil fuel, or a cotton plant, with many workers and manufacturing and transportation processes along the way.

Most synthetic threads like polyester are made from petroleum, a nonrenewable resource that even during the refining process produces contaminants. Synthetic fabrics and clothing are durable and relatively nondestructible, which means they don't easily degrade. Some companies accept used synthetic clothing for reuse as feedstock in their new synthetic blend fabrics.

When choosing clothing, check the labels and consider limiting clothes that require dry cleaning. The word *clean* is relative when you consider the chemicals left in your clothing that reach far beyond the closet. The traditional dry-cleaning process uses some of the harshest solvents with a little water to remove soil from dirty clothes. The solvent most often used by dry cleaners is perchloroethylene, known in the industry as perc. When spilled on the ground, perc leaches into groundwater. Because it is denser than water, it sinks in the aquifer, making remediation costly and complicated.

Perc is also released into the air during the cleaning process and is a hazardous air pollutant at certain levels. There are many green alternatives to dry cleaning today, including using carbon dioxide—the same gas that makes soda fizzy—under high pressure to clean clothes. Because the cleaning system relies on biodegradable silicone-based solvents, harmful chemicals don't linger on your clothes or in the environment.

PURE AND NATURAL

When looking for clothing that reduces wear and tear on the earth, consider natural and organic cotton, hemp, wool, and even bamboo. Many people wonder why wearing organic clothing should be a concern since no one is going to ingest it. However, what people wear does impact the environment.

The Tao of Cotton

Cotton has been used to make clothing for thousands of years. As with many other crops grown using conventional methods, pesticides are used to kill insects before they can cause damage. Large-scale agribusinesses now run the operations that depend on pesticides and fertilizers and include separating out the cotton fiber from the seed. The cotton fiber is used for clothing while the seeds take another route. Cottonseed oil is used in vegetable oil, salad dressings, and many processed foods like potato chips and snack crackers. Hulls are also used in cattle feed as high-protein fiber. The use of pesticides is fraught with environmental impact. Storm water runoff from rain flowing across cotton fields brings with it the residue and contamination left over from the chemicals.

It's estimated that cotton uses 53 million pounds of chemicals as pesticides, herbicides, and defoliants every year. Although cotton uses less than 3 percent of cultivated land, it uses about 11 percent of pesticides worldwide. More than 90 percent of the cotton grown today relies on chemicals, while 20 percent is grown from genetically modified seeds. Organic cotton represents only about 1 percent of the cotton grown worldwide. To avoid the problems that come with pesticides, researchers have genetically modified cotton plants to be pest-resistant. The most common transgenic cotton plant carries the *Bacillus thuringiensis* (Bt) gene. This gene kills caterpillars that feed on the cotton plant, stifling any damage. Transgenic cotton has been used all over the world by leading exporters such as China and India to increase prosperity by increasing production. However, there are skeptics who do not believe the increased production will last and that nature will find a way around the resistant cotton, eventually making stronger pesticides necessary.

The Organic Path

It is more expensive to grow cotton organically, but farmers are paid sufficiently to make up the difference. Organic cotton sells well, with extra money going back to the farmer. Large companies support the growing trend of organic cotton by promoting and selling lines of products made with organic cotton.

Organic cotton requires farmers to forgo using genetically modified seeds, chemical pesticides, and fertilizers. By going organic, the farmers no longer have to pay for expensive pesticides and receive a higher dollar value for their crop, sometimes bringing in twice as much. Organic cotton is a win-win situation for both the environment and the farmer.

Organic cotton also accounts for less than a tenth of a percent of all cotton harvested throughout the world, according to the US Department of Agriculture (USDA). However, demand for organic cotton is growing, and retailers are responding by incorporating more organic cotton into their clothing lines. In 2014/15, the organic cotton market was worth approximately $15.7 billion, according to Textile Exchange.

Organic cotton growers often use ladybugs and other natural enemies to combat pests. Pests are also handpicked from the plants. While this process takes much more time than applying chemicals, the farmers make up for it with the high prices they receive for their crops. Another important factor is that by eliminating pesticides from crops, workers are no longer exposed to dangerous chemicals. Studies have shown that the houses of farmworkers routinely contain pesticides brought home from the field, exposing the family members who live there.

Heavenly Hemp

Hemp, the nondrug form of cannabis, suffers from its association with marijuana. However, it is environmentally friendly. It does not require pesticides and, because the plants grow so densely, herbicides are not required either.

Over the centuries, hemp was commonly used to make sails on ships, leading experts to believe that the word *canvas* actually originated from the word *cannabis*, or kannabis, as it was spelled then. From masts to sails, hemp was used to make clothing, shoes, and even paper for maps. For decades it was a favorite of industry and farmers were encouraged to grow the crop because it had so many uses. Recreational use of hemp didn't become popular until the early twentieth century. The US government didn't even initially back the illegality of hemp and, in 1942, distributed 400,000 pounds of seed for farmers, including 4-H groups, to grow hemp in support of the war effort.

For more information on the history of hemp, check out *The Emperor Wears No Clothes* by Jack Herer. Published in 2000, this book gives readers a rundown on the politics of why hemp was outlawed and the powers that keep it out of reach. Experts agree Herer took hemp out of the closet and put it back on the table as a viable textile.

Even with legislation against its use, hemp never went away. Scientists who continued to study it found it to be lower in saturated fats than other vegetable oils. Still, growing the plant in much of the United States, even for industrial purposes, is unlawful. Hemp must be imported, usually from China, Romania, Hungary, and Poland, which is why it carries a higher price tag. It also doesn't benefit from the subsidies that other domestic textiles receive.

The Wisdom of Wool

Wool is a renewable and sustainable fabric, but problems abound with conventionally grown wool. As with cows, when sheep are raised in small, overgrazed pastures, they become vulnerable to parasites. To combat the pests, the sheep are dipped, literally, in pesticides. These dipping vats are walk-through troughs placed in pastures. The pesticides are toxic to fish and amphibians and are suspected endocrine disruptors.

When chemicals escape the vats, they contaminate groundwater and surface water and are capable of bioaccumulating in wildlife. Workers responsible for dipping sheep have become sick, and chemicals have been linked to nerve damage.

Alpacas are camel-like animals that are smaller than llamas. These gentle animals graze in herds in the Andes. The Suri alpaca grows long, silky dreadlocks, a favorite of spinners. Alpaca wool contains no lanolin and is truly hypoallergenic. Alpacas come in more than twenty different colors but are bred white for ease in dyeing.

Wool's chemical dependency continues with manufacturing. Wool is often washed and treated with formaldehydes and dioxins. Newer technologies even incorporate chlorine oxidation and silver backwashing to prevent shrinking.

Organically raised sheep live in pastures without pesticides and are not dipped. Healthy sheep are able to fend off parasites, making dipping unnecessary. Organic wool yarn is not chemically treated, but washed using biodegradable soap. While some people may be allergic to lanolin, oil that naturally occurs in wool, wool in itself is nonallergenic. It's also naturally fire retardant, making it safer than treated clothing. Natural wool clothing is breathable but is a good insulator. It's durable and wrinkle resistant and can be dyed and spun into a variety of fabrics.

Close to Nirvana: Bamboo

Bamboo is a quick-growing grass. Two of its more redeeming qualities are that it removes dangerous carbon dioxide from the air as part of photosynthesis and that it can be harvested relatively quickly, meaning smaller amounts of land are needed to grow it. Bamboo doesn't require fertilizers or pesticides and is hypoallergenic. To date, there hasn't been any genetically modified bamboo used in the apparel process. The fiber produced from bamboo is moisture-wicking and antimicrobial. Clothing made from bamboo is colorfast and can be washed as if it were cotton clothing.

A Meditation on Silk

Silk is a protein fiber spun by moth larvae. It can be considered a renewable resource and is biodegradable; however, traditional harvesting and processing methods don't comply with everyone's idea of planet friendly. The majority of silk seen in the United States comes from China, Korea, Japan, and India. The silk production process uses Bombyx mori caterpillar or larvae, which attach themselves to the leaves of mulberry trees and begin spinning.

The cocoon is finished in about two days and contains one continuous silk strand that can measure thousands of feet long. If left alone, the larvae would continue through the pupa stage and then emerge from the cocoon as a moth, but it would break the silk strand in the process. To maintain the continuous thread, cocoons are usually steamed, boiled, or baked to kill the larvae inside. The cocoons are then opened and the silk unfurled. The thread is washed or degummed using alkaline washes. It takes an estimated 25,000 cocoons to produce 1 pound of silk thread. This harvesting process is highly labor intensive and commonly relies on low-wage workers.

There are a few companies that offer silk while working to improve one or more aspects of the harvesting process. Both Peace Silk and Ahimsa Peace Silk allow the larvae to continue to grow inside the cocoons, requiring the threads broken by the moth's emergence to be spun back together.

THE PATH FROM FIBERS TO FABRIC

Fibers from both natural and manufactured materials are made into fabric at mills. Cooperatives work with brands, retailers, and farmers to match organic fibers with mills and brands. To be certified organic, a mill must be cleaned of residues. If a farmer's crop is small, a mill won't stop work to clean the equipment, and independent farmers have difficulty finding a mill. By working with cooperatives, farmers are able to combine their volume, making it more profitable for the mills to process their cotton. The farmers then have a better chance of selling their crops. Also, more and more brands are incorporating organic fiber lines and working with organic farmers to purchase their feedstock.

RESPONSIBLE MANUFACTURING

Clothing manufacturers can help the environment by implementing sustainable designs and operations. By working toward using renewable energy and increasing energy efficiency, achieving improved health and safety for employees and the public, and addressing waste disposal and reclamation within the manufacturing process, companies can positively impact their neighborhoods and surrounding communities.

THE ENLIGHTENED WAY: REUSING AND RECYCLING

In northern California, women business owners are forgoing the traditional costly consignment store overhead and instead holding weekend sales in neighborhoods and popular local gathering sites, such as fairgrounds, all featuring the new and slightly used styles of the season at a fraction of the cost. Shoppers save on cost while also extending the resources used during the initial manufacturing process.

Reincarnated Fabrics

Rather than recycling an entire garment, many items can be recycled for parts. An old pair of jeans can be sacrificed for parts to save another pair, a patch here, a pocket there. Denim and other fabrics can also be kept for handmade projects like purses, pillows, and blankets. Old T-shirts from concerts or sport teams can be patched together to make a memorable quilt. Before tossing that shrunken T-shirt or those threadbare jeans, consider whether they could be reincarnated in a different form.

A number of designers are incorporating used clothing into their designs. Material is used as-is and isn't reprocessed. It may be cut and stitched and incorporated into a design with other recycled fabrics. This industry is still in its infancy, with limited retail lines.

Manufacturers are also incorporating recycling activities, using clothing that is no longer in use, postconsumer waste, and material waste from processing (also known as postindustrial waste). Postconsumer waste is material that would more than likely end up in a landfill or at the incinerator. Removing it from the waste stream saves landfill space, air quality, and other degradation caused by common disposal practices. Recycling postindustrial waste is beneficial to the economy and the environment.

Using recycled material saves energy because incorporating recycled material into feedstock reduces the energy needed for manufacturing. The energy needed to obtain and transport raw materials is reduced as well. In addition, fewer natural resources are needed when recycled material is incorporated.

Some companies use recycled plastic bottles and 100 percent cotton to create a 50/50 cotton/poly blend. The fabric is used to make T-shirts, caps, and visors. Clothing and hats can be purchased plain or screened with predesigned eco-friendly messages.

Clothes brought into a mill for recycling are sorted into material types with different end uses. Pants and skirts can be shredded and used for fillers in car insulation and furniture padding. Wool clothing can be reclaimed to make yarn or fabric. Cotton and silk can be recycled to make cloth rags and even paper. Denim can be recycled into insulation for buildings to improve energy efficiency.

Walking a Peaceful Path: Shoes

When considering what materials and chemicals go into your wardrobe, don't forget to look down. Shoe manufacturing is heavily dependent on dyes, glues, chemically tanned leather, and rubber. The industry as a whole has been slow to incorporate more sustainable practices and improve environmental welfare.

Hemp is a sustainable fabric used to make a variety of shoes from sandals and clogs to dress shoes and sneakers. It's durable and it breathes, giving feet fresh air. Sustainable rubber is now also being used, but it may not, in the end, contribute to a sustainable environment. Processing rubber is extensive and includes compounding and mixing, milling and calendaring (a finishing process used on textiles), extruding, coating, cooling and cutting, building, vulcanizing, and grinding. Each step in the process generates emissions, wastewater, and solid waste material. Heavy metals are a primary chemical component and waste product of making rubber. Sustainable practices take into account healthy harvesting of the trees and proper handling of wastes. As efficient processing methods expand, using recycled or reprocessed rubber to make flip-flops and soles for sneakers is also becoming more common.

Leather is largely garnered from factory farming of cows and pigs. The process used to transform the animals' skin into the leather seen in the stores depends largely on a mix of harmful chemicals. After cows are slaughtered, salt is used to cure and preserve the skin. This is usually done at the meat-processing facility, and then the cured skin is shipped out for tanning. Any remaining flesh and hair are removed using a lime solution. The liming chemicals are then removed by neutralizing them with an acidic rinse. The process used to tan the leather depends on the leather's end use. Softer leather for purses and shoes uses a mineral or chrome tanning wash. Stiffer leather for luggage or furniture uses a vegetable tanning process. Shoppers looking to purchase leather products can consider fair trade organizations that rely on free-range cattle and good working conditions for those processing the hides. The life of shoes can be extended by having them repaired rather than replaced. Not only does this support a local business; it also saves natural resources.

Purses, wallets, belts, and jewelry—as with other leather items—take advantage of leather's longevity. Many purses incorporate organic and recycled materials. Take into consideration the fact that big-name manufacturers generally control much of the market without encouraging sustainable practices.

Illuminated Jewelry

Diamonds may be the ultimate gift to receive in some corners, but unless your rock comes from a certified source, the tragic cost of human labor and rape of the earth is a crime—and you'll carry that negative impact with you...literally. In order to mine diamonds, the land surface is scraped clean and a pit is dug to access the diamond deposits. Waste is generated as trees and cover materials are hoisted aside, dirt and rocks are excavated, and mine tailings are generated. Depending on the environmental laws in the area, the mine may be reclaimed after the diamonds are gone, but it is impossible to restore it to natural conditions.

Consider purchasing eco-friendly jewelry. Many organizations carry jewelry made of silver and other bright gemstones made by small organizations in an effort to promote sustainability. Others promote the use of recycled gold.

CHAPTER SEVEN

The Pure Outdoors

*In our haste to maintain a perfect yard, we can forget that
the outdoors is a source of personal energy, there to soothe our souls
through duty and care. If you focus on the patterns formed as you push
the lawn mower, it's amazing what you may discover between and
around the blades of grass. Putting your hands in the soil—
earth-touching—can discharge your worries. Let them flow
through your fingertips to be absorbed by the earth.*

Consider that your home is your own, private ecosystem, starting with your landscaping and hardscapes. It's your opportunity to exercise some green control, recognizing that the products you use—such as pesticides and lawn care products—can, and do, impact the environment far beyond your property line.

With some simple tips and wise consumer choices, a green garden and yard can be the envy of the neighborhood—and a place of quiet contemplation for you.

MINDFUL MOWING?

Lawns are getting greener, and it's not just the fertilizer. Taking the environment into account when choosing ground cover and mowing options has become an important issue when it comes to maintaining a healthy yard.

A Conscious Choice: Ground Cover

Low-maintenance yards can also be low cost while providing a variety of texture to enhance your outdoor living. Choosing a low-maintenance lawn can also reduce the impact your lawn has on the environment and the amount of natural resources used. Lawns can be planted with a mixture of native tall grasses or plants that require little maintenance. Prairie grasses and flowers will grow taller than standard lawn grass and will beautify the yard with colorful flowers during different times of the year. Other plants and flowers can be added to offer decorative alternatives to grass and give lawns a wilder and less manicured look. Short-growing plants and ground cover can provide an alternative to standard grass while allowing people to walk and play in the yard. The right grass substitute or no-mow lawn can reduce and possibly even eliminate the need to mow and fertilize altogether. Multiple companies offer seed mixes of wildflowers and shortgrasses that can be thrown in the yard. Mixtures can be made according to geographic location, watering and lighting requirements, mowing needs, and soil conditions. These mixtures include ingredients like ryegrass, clover, daisies, lavender, and thyme. Some of the companies that provide no-mow lawn and grass alternatives are listed here:

- Pro Time Lawn Seed (formerly Hobbs & Hopkins Ltd.) is located in Oregon and carries seed mixes like Fleur de Lawn and Herb de Lawn that are especially for the Pacific Northwest. They work closely with Oregon State University to determine different ecology mixes for lawns and gardens. You can visit their website at https://ptlawnseed.com/.

- No Mow Grass can be ordered online from the website www.nomowgrass.com. They carry specific seed mixes amenable to the variety of weather conditions in the United States. The website also offers preparation and planting instructions. No Mow Grass carries wildflower seed mixes for all types of weather conditions.

- Prairie Nursery provides seed mixes for the northern United States and parts of Canada. Their seed mixes include prairie plants and grasses. They also carry lawn mixes that include slow-growing, fine fescue grass, which grows up to 9 inches tall. Due to their slender build, the blades fall over, giving them a height of about 4 inches. Fescue grasses are good for areas that are too warm for cool-weather grass and too cool for warm-weather grass. Check out the mixtures at www.prairienursery.com.

- Wildflower Farm carries a variety of tall prairie grasses and shorter lawn grasses. Their stock is more applicable to the central-northern United States. They carry Eco-Lawn, a substitute for standard yards that includes a mixture of seven fescue grasses. Visit their website at www.wildflowerfarm.com.

- Stepables, a brand of creeping perennials, are carried in a variety of lawn and garden shops across the United States. Stepables were created by the Under A Foot Plant Company. They offer a wealth of plants that can be selected by zone (location within the United States) at their website, www.stepables.com. Information on each plant includes a photo, sunlight and watering requirements, information on whether mowing is necessary, and other maintenance requirements.

Maintaining a healthy lawn is even easier if you use native plants when landscaping. Native plants are adapted to local climates and conditions, so they don't need a lot of care to thrive—they have been flourishing for years without any help from humans. They are accustomed to local pests, so native plants do not depend on pesticides. Native plants are also acclimated to local weather conditions and rainfall, meaning they don't need excessive watering or protection. Local birds and butterflies are often attracted to native species, making a yard a haven to animals. Native plants will also live longer than exotics, saving time and money and conserving natural resources.

Ultimately, using native plants will cut down on the effort and energy needed to maintain a beautiful lawn.

In the southern and southwestern United States, xeriscape landscaping is a very popular alternative to high-maintenance yards. Xeriscaping uses plants specifically selected for their drought-resistant qualities. In areas where water restrictions are common, these types of plants offer a pleasant alternative to standard lawns. One example is the use of clover instead of grass. Not only is clover drought-resistant; it's tolerant of weeds and insects, requires minimal mowing, and offers a soft cushion for walking.

Enlightened Mowers

The impact of traditional gas-fueled lawn mowers on air quality is driving consumers to re-evaluate their choices, driving the manufacturers to increase the range of consumer-powered models offered just a few years ago.

The California Air Resources Board (CARB) estimates that 2006 model lawn mowers emit 93 times more emissions than 2006 model cars. California is working toward legislation that would require emission standards to be more stringent than those in the other forty-nine US states. Lawn mower manufacturers may soon have two lines of mowers, one compliant with California requirements and the other meeting broader requirements for the rest of the country.

If you want to skip a trip to the gym, mow your yard using a reel lawn mower. Reel mowers are the oldest type of residential lawn mowers. The blades are attached to the wheels, so pushing the mower manually causes the wheels to roll and the blades to rotate, cutting the grass. While some people may choose this type of mower for nostalgic reasons, others may like its simplicity—no engines or ignitions to keep in working order and no fuel mixture to store in the garage. Because they are not dependent on fuel, reel lawn mowers don't produce any emissions.

Electric lawn mowers work well for small yards and gardens. Although they do not produce any emissions, these mowers do get their power from local plants that may burn fossil fuels. Not only are electric mowers friendly for air quality; they're quiet. Some can be equipped with a grass catcher and even have mulch capabilities. Electric mowers are lightweight, and the handles can be folded for easy storage. Cordless mowers can be charged overnight to provide up to forty minutes of mowing time the next day.

Newer power-driven lawn mowers are more efficient than older models, but they can still produce smog-forming chemicals and carbon monoxide. Lawn mowers do not have catalytic converters, which are required on automobiles to treat the exhaust fume before it escapes and to remove nitrogen oxides, volatile organic compounds, and hydrocarbons before they can combine with sunlight to form smog. The EPA is currently working on legislation that would require the installation of catalytic converters in lawn mowers.

Leaves and grass clippings need not be taken to the curb. They can be used in compost and made into mulch or used in planting beds and gardens. The EPA estimates that up to 31 million tons of yard waste is collected, transported, and processed by municipalities every year. Keeping yard trimmings at home for use in the garden reduces waste processing and the need for transportation. If raking isn't your ideal pastime, manual leaf sweepers are available. Some companies offer an assortment of lawn sweepers that can be used to collect leaves from yards, sidewalks, and driveways, ready to put in the compost pile.

SAVING GREEN ON GREEN

When it comes to taking care of the lawn, there are plenty of options and alternatives for eliminating pests and maintaining a healthy stand of grass or ground cover.

Unhealthy grass and plants are more susceptible to pests. Before turning to pesticides to control bugs, work on getting your plants in shape. One way to pump up plants and get rid of garbage at the same time is to compost.

Turning Over a New Leaf

Compost is made of recycled food scraps, yard trimmings, clean paper, and even ashes from your fireplace. Don't include meat, pet droppings, or oil and grease because they can attract rodents that can carry disease and can kill beneficial organisms. Commercial compost units can be purchased from lawn and garden centers, online companies, or even through local extension or utility offices. Compost units can also be made at home using materials like chicken wire, bricks, or buckets. The organic material in the compost bin needs to be turned and watered regularly to mix the contents from the inner portions of the pile to the outer portions. The material in the center of the pile decays as it is kept warm and moist, a perfect atmosphere for degradation. When the mixture turns into a dark brown crumbly material that smells like the earth, it's ready to go.

Using compost is a great way to improve soil texture and keep weeds from growing. It increases air and water absorption in the soil and can be used as mulch in the lawn or garden. Compost makes great potting soil.

By joining a group of local growers, green gardeners can exchange information and find out what is working and what is not. Organic gardening has grown in popularity, so joining a group either in person or online is easy. Extension offices or local garden clubs may have information on groups or meetings in your area.

Beneficial insects and other animals can be very, well, beneficial when it comes to getting rid of pests in your garden. Ladybugs, lacewings, and ground beetles feed on aphids, chinch bugs, and weevils. Lizards, birds, and frogs will likely make a meal out of pesky caterpillars and grubs. But they will not be attracted by the pests alone and sometimes need to be enticed by their favorite plants. Adding bordering flowers will attract beneficial insects by providing shelter and nectar. Not only will there be fewer pests; the beneficial bugs will also help pollinate flowers, fruits, and vegetables.

When it comes to countering an invasion in the garden, concerned gardeners may need a more hands-on approach to get rid of weeds and pests. Caterpillars, worms, and beetles can be picked off plants and destroyed. Mixing a few tablespoons of a strong-smelling ingredient like cayenne, garlic, or horseradish with a quart of water and spraying it on plants can drive away some pests. There are also recipes for mildew and fungi treatments that include common kitchen ingredients like baking soda and vinegar.

Here are three simple recipes:

1. Mix 3 tablespoons of natural apple cider vinegar with 1 gallon of water. Spray on plants during the cool part of the day.
2. Mix 1 teaspoon of baking soda, one drop of dishwashing detergent, and 1 tablespoon of canola oil in 1 gallon of water; spray the mixture on plants to treat fungus and mildew.
3. Soak chopped garlic overnight in 1 pint of mineral oil. Strain the mixture to remove the garlic; then add 1 pint of water and no more than $\frac{1}{2}$ teaspoon of soap remains. Spray the mixture directly on pest infestations. To make sure that plants won't be adversely affected, use home remedies on just a portion of the plants first.

PESTICIDE TRANSPARENCY

Rachel Carson's *Silent Spring* educated the world on the dangers of pesticides. The book focuses on the use of pesticides and their impact on the web of life. Pesticides often harm more animals than intended. Targeted animals absorb the pesticide, and then a second, unintended animal eats the first and ingests the poison, bringing both populations down. Carson's work highlighted the importance of understanding the impacts of chemicals on the environment. New pesticides developed through green chemistry are designed to target specific organisms and will not harm any other living systems.

The EPA has banned the manufacture and use of a number of pesticides previously considered safe. This list includes chlorinated hydrocarbon insecticides such as aldrin and dieldrin. It also includes common pesticides like chlordane, lindane, and toxaphene, which were used as flea control on animals. This is only a portion of the chemicals that can be detected in the tissues of animals and people after the chemicals have been removed from use. Carson's critics claim that without pesticides, civilization would return to the dark ages when insects ran rampant and disease was uncontrolled. However, the impacts of many synthetic pesticides are still unknown because many of the effects are long term. The overuse of pesticides has been acknowledged, and individuals, corporations, and municipalities have taken proper application more seriously. People have begun to appreciate chemicals' destructive power and are using more safety precautions and following directions more closely.

The EPA registers pesticides for use on the basis that they do not pose unreasonable risks to people or the environment. Unfortunately, the long-term and synergistic effects are not always known when the chemicals are registered.

The pesticide market is highly competitive; companies are developing new and proprietary compounds every day. It's true that pesticides have allowed an abundance of crops to be grown and incidences of certain diseases to be reduced. When pesticides are used as directed, they can prove beneficial in preventing illness and even death. Pesticides are known to kill bugs that carry diseases like malaria and West Nile virus. They are also praised by the farming community for improving crop health and production by eliminating damaging pests.

CHAPTER EIGHT

The Zen-Fully Green Consumer

The green consumer is one who, in Zen tradition, takes the right action the first time. That means purchasing products packaged in Earth-friendly containers that can be easily recycled for another purpose. It is enlightened to use the power of your money to influence and encourage manufacturers to take mindful right action as well.

Being a good consumer is generally defined as being a buyer and pumping money into the economy. Your patronage generates a need for services and manufacturing, which creates jobs and benefits everyone. But there can be a downside to consumerism too. Many products are not manufactured with environmental responsibility in mind. As production goes up, so does its impact on the environment. This can be especially true if keeping costs low is the greatest factor in producing anything, from sweatshirts to picture frames.

When shopping, consider not just the quantity but the quality of what you buy. The cheapest product isn't always the best choice. Are you buying from conscientious companies? Were the products made from sustainable practices? Every purchase is a vote, and you as a consumer wield more power than you may think. Being a good consumer means thinking about the impact of what you buy, both economically and environmentally.

The US Bureau of Labor Statistics calculated that purchasing power has tripled since 1901. Why and how did this happen? A change to a consumer goods–oriented economy combined with mass consumption was brought about by the onslaught of advertising and the availability of credit.

Although there's no harm in enjoying life, it can be worthwhile to trim the excess in an effort to lead a greener life. Fossil fuels are an important ingredient in the production of just about anything, from forming the plastic to transporting the product to market, so cutting back even a little can have an impact.

The Essence of Manufacturing

Conscientious manufacturers keep the environment in mind when designing products and deciding how to package and transport them. Businesses can also modify their products and methods for more sustainable production.

Sustainable business programs and practices are more prevalent in Europe and countries like Australia and New Zealand, but greener practices are starting to make headway in the United States as well. On a state level, Wisconsin, California, and Oregon have recycled packaging laws on their books. These states require that all rigid plastic containers sold contain 25 percent recycled content. This encourages manufacturers across the country to achieve the mandated content to avoid having to produce different packages for different states. Legislation levels the playing field for all types of businesses, making everyone play by the same rules. Successful regulations often set goals or standards, and programs are established to encourage companies to achieve or even go beyond compliance.

A Sustainable Mantra: Reduce, Reuse, and Recycle

Few practices are more Zen than the three Rs. They're the key to living a more eco-friendly life and reducing the amount of waste you generate. Many people include recycling in their everyday affairs, taking glass, paper, and plastic to the curb or a recycling center. Reusing and reducing mean thinking about purchases and ways to minimize the impact of waste on the environment.

Righteous Reduction

Consider these tips to help reduce what you bring home:

- Make a list and check it twice. Whether you're shopping for groceries, school supplies, makeup, or home repair items, sticking with a list will avoid unnecessary or impulse purchases. Preparing an accurate list may take some time, but consider that time an investment in the future.
- Avoid the just-in-case purchase. If you aren't sure you need something, just assume you don't. Being organized at home can help you know what you have in stock.
- Think about where the new purchase will go and what it will displace. A new blender may be a wonderful treat, but if the old one still works, is it necessary to buy a new one? If a new one is in order, can the old one be donated or recycled?
- Evaluate want versus need. It can be worth the extra thought to consider whether a purchase is for something you need or want. If it's just a desire, can it be quelled?
- Beware of bargains. Bargains are designed to move merchandise, not necessarily to save you money.
- Beware of warehouses. That 25-pound bag of flour may seem like a good deal, but if it ends up getting thrown away, then it's not.
- Walk to the store. You'll buy only what you can easily carry.

Active Reuse

It's truly common sense: Pack your peanut butter and jelly sandwich in a reusable container instead of that plastic wrap you'll discard immediately. Carry the drink of your choice in a (safe) plastic bottle instead of relying on multiple one-use cups throughout the day. Reusing not only avoids the production of new items; it also cuts down on the wasteful products you consume. It eliminates waste that will likely be disposed of in a landfill or incinerated.

There are a lot of other ways to reuse materials by taking small steps that can be incorporated into your life a little at a time. Here are a few for starters:

- Reuse totes and bags. When going shopping, take along your own bags. This pairs reducing with recycling—you'll reduce the need for plastic bags and reuse the canvas or cloth bags you already have.

- Swap it out. Many cities today have networks to exchange one person's trash for someone else's treasure. This is also popular on the Internet—members post messages describing what they have available and other members post their interest. Members schedule a pickup, but no money trades hands. One dominant force in the swap arena is Freecycle. See www.freecycle.org for more information.

- Make a charitable donation. If you know of an organization in your area that's looking for household items, clothes, or other goods (cell phones, for instance), consider making a donation. Sometimes organizations offer to pick up the items, and donations are often tax deductible.

- Be creative. Printer paper has two sides and can be reused as scrap paper. Packaging materials can be used for arts and crafts projects. Sunday comics make colorful wrapping paper. Junk mail can be cut and used as notepaper.

Reincarnated Recyclables

Recycled materials have now become a part of the processing stream, taking the place of virgin materials in manufacturing. Manufacturing with recycled materials conserves raw materials and reduces energy consumption. Here's where it really counts: It takes 95 percent less energy to produce an aluminum can from recycled aluminum than from bauxite ore. Making a glass bottle from recycled glass uses 40 percent less energy than making one from sand, soda ash, and limestone. Recycled newsprint uses 40 percent less energy than making newsprint from trees, although paper mills get power from scrap wood while most recycling mills rely on conventional power sources.

The Container Recycling Institute estimated that in 2014, 80 percent of plastic water bottles are never recycled. Thirty-eight million go into landfills each year, where they can take up to seven hundred years to dissolve.

The recycling loop includes three steps: collecting recyclable materials, physically recycling the materials, and purchasing items made from recycled materials. Keep the recycling containers in a convenient location, possibly in or close to the kitchen. You may not be consistent early on, but eventually recycling will become a habit that you incorporate into your everyday tasks. Common products containing recycled content include paper towels, carpeting, egg cartons, and motor oil.

Plastics

Plastic bottles are everywhere from the refrigerator to the laundry room, each with an arrowed triangle and number stamped on the bottom. The numbers associated with recycled plastic can be confusing, so here's the rundown:

- No. 1 plastic is polyethylene terephthalate, also known as PETE or PET. It's used for soda bottles and other food containers. PETE can be recycled into fiberfill for pillows and sleeping bags and other food and drink containers.
- No. 2 plastic is high-density polyethylene, or HDPE. Milk jugs are made from nonpigmented HDPE; laundry detergent bottles are manufactured using pigmented, or colored, HDPE. If separated well, these plastics can be recycled into the same color bottles and jugs.
- No. 3 plastic is polyvinyl chloride, or PVC. It's used to make PVC pipe and medical tubing. Orange traffic cones and garden hoses are also usually made out of recycled PVC.
- No. 4 plastic is low-density polyethylene, commonly referred to as LDPE. It's used to make squeeze bottles for condiments like jelly and ketchup. LDPE can be recycled into landscape timber and garbage-can liners.
- No. 5 plastic is polypropylene, or PP. It's used for storing food like yogurt and can be recycled into a variety of items from medicine bottles to battery cables.
- No. 6 plastic is polystyrene. It's used to make meat trays used by grocery stores along with plastic cups and plates.

When recycled, polystyrene is turned into foam packing and license plate frames.

- No. 7 plastic incorporates all other plastics not included in the first six categories. It's used to make large water bottles and plastic lumber.

Metals

Talk about a turnaround—aluminum cans are now one of the easiest items to recycle. From the time a can is turned in for recycling, it will take only about sixty days for it to be sorted, cleaned, processed, filled, and back on a store shelf.

A variety of aluminum products can be recycled including pots, pans, and even baseball bats. Once recycled, aluminum sheets and forged aluminum can be used to make drink cans, car parts, and construction materials. Aluminum can also be made into a powder and used for a variety of products like explosives and decorating materials.

Paper

Like other materials, paper is sorted and baled in a recycling facility. Bales of flattened cardboard and bales of mixed paper and newsprint are sold to mills for processing. According to the Paper Industry Association Council, 86 percent of Americans have access to curbside or drop-off paper recycling programs. More than 50 percent of the paper used is recycled. Every ton of paper that is recycled saves 3.3 cubic yards of space in a landfill.

Electronic Waste—A Karmic Nightmare

One of the largest concerns of recycling today is managing electronic waste. E-waste includes cell phones, computers, TVs, VCRs, copiers, and fax machines—anything with a battery or a plug. While some of this equipment can be recycled or donated to a charity, much of it is obsolete or broken.

More than 3,000 tons of electronic equipment are discarded every day. Computers contain a multitude of parts, and some include enough lead and mercury to be considered hazardous. When taken to a landfill for disposal, e-waste takes up valuable room. Worse, it has the potential to release metals such as mercury and lead into the environment, although placing e-waste in a landfill is healthier for the environment than incineration. When incinerated, the plastics release dioxins into the air. The only national legislation regarding e-waste applies to cathode ray tubes (CRT) from computer and TV monitors. This legislation states that CRT will not be considered solid waste when processed for recycling. This act saves recyclers from having to abide by strict solid waste regulations and keeps the waste from being considered hazardous. But because it affects only one component of the volume of e-waste generated, it doesn't really help the e-waste recycling industry as a whole.

Some states have enacted legislation to address the growing problem of e-waste and e-waste recycling. California assesses an advance recovery fee when electronics are purchased. The amount of the fee varies from $6 to $10, and goes into an account that's used to pay collectors and recyclers.

An important concern with the recycling of e-waste is that portions of waste that are generated in the United States are now shipped to China and India for recycling. This has huge transportation costs, financially and environmentally. However, as these countries become overburdened by waste and citizens rally for stronger environmental laws, it is expected that exporting e-waste from the United States will be limited.

A more malicious problem is e-waste that is shipped to developing countries under the guise of technological donations. As much as 75 percent of the donated products do not work, according to a speech by the executive director of the UN Environment Programme. The defunct products end up in landfills, where dangerous pollutants leak out and contaminate the soil and water. Other items take up relatively small portions of the waste stream but should be recycled nonetheless:

- Single-use and rechargeable batteries are accepted by some radio electronics and office stores.
- Carpet and padding can be used to make other carpet and padding. Ask if your old carpet will be recycled.
- Car parts such as batteries, used oil, and oil filters can usually be dropped off at local auto-part stores for no charge.
- Printer, fax, and inkjet cartridges can be recycled. There are many fundraising programs available for collecting and reimbursing for these recyclables. You can also send old cartridges back to the manufacturer.

- Cell phones can be returned to your service provider to be reused or recycled.

- Some electronics stores will take your old materials for recycling. Call local stores to find out whether they will allow you to drop off your old electronics for recycling.

- For locations of other recycling organizations, see www.earth911.org for a directory.

GARBAGE: A PSYCHIC AND PHYSICAL DRAIN

The EPA reports that over the past forty years the amount of waste generated for each person has increased from 2.7 to 4.6 pounds per day. This adds up to over 236 million tons of municipal solid waste annually in the United States, double what was thrown away in 1980. States are now obligated to enforce either federal regulations or more stringent local laws for managing garbage. All solid waste facilities—including both landfills and incinerators—are permitted by state or federal agencies and are required to be operated according to applicable laws.

The Life of a Landfill

Most discarded waste is disposed of in landfills with strict guidelines for construction, operation, and closure when the landfill has reached its allowable height. The groundwater, surface water, and air around the facility must be monitored, even if the facility is no longer operating.

As waste decomposes in a landfill, it produces a liquid called leachate. The leachate drains through the waste and collects on a liner of plastic sheeting in the bottom of the landfill. Leachate is usually pumped to storage tanks at the landfill facility and is later either pumped or trucked to a wastewater treatment plant. Because little was known about what happened when waste degraded, older landfills were not required to have bottom liners, and the leachate was able to migrate into the ground where it contaminated groundwater or surface water.

Decomposition also produces methane, a dangerous greenhouse gas. Methane can be collected through piping and used to generate electricity; however, there is a limited time in landfill life when this is economically feasible as methane generation peaks and then decreases. Vents are constructed on top of landfills that go into the waste and allow the gas to either disperse into the air or be collected and burned. The size of the landfill and the volume of gas produced dictate how methane is handled.

Bioreactor landfills, a recent advance in solid waste, have piping and pumps that recirculate the leachate from the bottom of the landfill back to the top so it can again drain through the waste. This practice provides liquid that microorganisms need to degrade the waste, speeding up the process of decay and allowing the waste to settle or become more compact in less time. Because landfill height is one of the limiting factors for operation, compacting the waste allows for more garbage to be buried within the landfill. The number of landfills has decreased over time, but their size has increased. Finding a place to construct a landfill is difficult because it doesn't make a pleasant neighbor. So rather than try to locate new landfills, municipalities are choosing to expand the landfills they already have. Instead of operating a landfill, many municipalities would rather send their waste to other counties or even to other states.

The Burn of Burning

About 14 percent of collected solid waste goes to incinerators where it's burned at very high temperatures, which destroys bacteria and certain chemicals. However, incineration also produces air contaminants like nitrogen oxides, sulfur dioxides, mercury compounds, dioxins, and carbon dioxide. The composition of the waste incinerated affects the types and quantities of compounds emitted. Pollution equipment is required at all incinerators, but strict adherence to operations must be maintained for the incinerator and pollution equipment to work properly.

Ash is produced as part of the incineration process. Bottom ash, the remnants of the burned material, remains in the incinerator. Fly ash is lighter particulate matter that floats up the stack of the incinerator. Both types of ash are usually disposed of in landfills, which is a concern for workers and nearby residents because it can be difficult to manage the light material. Contamination is also a concern because it can trickle from the ash into the leachate and potentially into the groundwater and surface water. Backyard burning isn't such a great idea either, and many communities are banning the practice. Unless the waste is burned in an incinerator, the high temperatures needed to safely break down dangerous chemicals won't be reached, which could cause the release of chemicals like dioxin. For a safer alternative, try composting.

Waste-to-energy plants generate power from garbage that is incinerated and use the heat to generate steam and produce electricity. Construction of these plants is very expensive, but as the cost of energy continues to rise and space for new landfills becomes harder to find, these facilities may become a more popular disposal approach.

CHAPTER NINE

Raising Enlightened Children

Zen is about rediscovery and often uses the term beginner's mind *as a way to describe the open state of mind that's necessary to experience new things without the judgments we often use as adults. Children (beginners) are more open to possibility and experience new things with all senses.*

Being a parent is a great opportunity to set in motion a new, planet-friendly means of existence. By using the eight tools of Zen enlightenment, you can teach your children the value of their choice, the value of their action, and the value of their impact on the planet. What could be a more worthy goal?

BABIES

The number, type, and variety of baby products available have increased exponentially over the last few generations. Along with new clothes, gear, and utensils, books on raising babies line the shelves and magazines and websites are full of informative articles. This onslaught of information and alternatives comes at a time when parents may already feel overwhelmed. Trying to lead an eco-conscious life doesn't have to happen overnight. Parents can take a deep breath, tackle items or concerns one by one, and then get ready to improvise.

The Journey to Solids

After six months of breast milk (the greenest food on Earth), babies may be ready for some solid food. The first solid food babies usually get their lips around is cereal. Some parents may choose to make their own baby food rather than rely on store-bought brands.

Cereal can either be purchased in a box or made at home. Generally, when you purchase cereal, all that's required is adding a little milk, formula, or water. Homemade cereal is a little more time-consuming, but you can make it in batches and freeze for easy use later. Ice cube trays can be used for freezing baby food; each cube measures out to be a serving size of approximately 1 ounce.

There are also commercially available baby food–freezing trays that are compartmentalized with lids. When making rice or oat cereal at home, the grains must be ground and cooked, unlike commercially made cereal that's already cooked and dehydrated before it's purchased.

If you are looking for baby food recipes and don't know where to turn, check out https://wholesomebabyfood.momtastic.com. This website contains recipes for your baby's beginning cereal and even more recipes for different stages up to one year. The site also has articles on other food-related issues and answers frequently asked questions.

From cereal and oats, parents can move on to feeding baby other foods like vegetables, fruits, and yogurt. Some foods can be mashed with a fork, like bananas, while other foods, like sweet potatoes, may need to be ground in a food processor or a baby-food grinder. Vegetables will need to be cooked before you grind them. As with cereal, foods can be made ahead of time in batches and frozen as individual servings in reusable trays. Making baby food at home eliminates the single-serve containers used to sell baby food and the environmental impacts from manufacturing and transporting all those little jars and pouches.

Compassionate Diapering

Cloth versus disposables becomes the question nightmares are made of. Some children are allergic to the dyes and fragrances in disposable diapers. Others may be sensitive to cloth diapers if they aren't changed quickly after they're soiled or if they're not washed well between uses. Diapers washed using a diaper service can reduce the potential for diaper rash when compared to home-washed nappies because services tend to use extremely hot water rather than chemical disinfectants.

Disposable diapers are made from cellulose and plastic. It's estimated that in the United States the manufacturing of disposable diapers uses up to 80,000 pounds of plastic and more than 250,000 trees every year. It's a highly industrialized process that results in the discharge of wastewater into rivers and streams and the release of dioxin into the air.

Disposable diapers make up about 1.3 percent of all the solid waste going into landfills today, and they're full of human waste that contains germs and viruses. When cloth diapers are washed, the solids are flushed down the toilet and treated with other waste at a proper wastewater facility. Landfills are not designed specifically to handle biological waste; however, when operated correctly, all liquid draining from a landfill is collected and disposed of at a wastewater treatment plant. More than the contents of the diapers, the volume of diapers and the ability to reduce any component of the waste stream going into a landfill is the concern. If diapers are incinerated, the chlorine bleach they contain is converted to dioxin, another mark in the negative column for disposables.

Then again, cloth diapers are not without their energy demands. While the amount of water needed to wash one dirty diaper can be considered negligible, its impact on water use and wastewater discharge can be significant when large quantities of diapers are taken into account. Diaper services enjoy water savings because large numbers of diapers are washed together, requiring less water per diaper. Where you live impacts the cost of a diaper service.

In areas where there is a high population of people who use a diaper service, the cost will be lower. In remote and more rural locations, the cost will likely be higher because delivery trucks will have to travel longer distances. In some areas, the cost of using a diaper service is lower than using disposable diapers; in other areas, it's more expensive. Diaper services have suffered from the rise in disposable diapers and negative advertising from the disposable diaper manufacturers, and as a result there are fewer services. However, as more parents become concerned with the environment, diaper services are back on the rise. Many parents compromise when it comes to diapering, using cloth diapers at home but opting for disposables when traveling and at night. Parents can opt for biodegradable and even flushable disposable diapers and inserts that draw urine away from the baby and make dumping solids much easier. Some biodegradable diapers are made with chlorine-free absorbent materials that don't contribute to the production of dioxin. Check the packaging for more information.

Cloth diapers have come a long way over the years. Pins can be used but are no longer necessary. Parents or caregivers can opt to use form-fitting covers with Velcro straps or all-in-one diapers that have Velcro straps right on the diapers. Parents can even choose between organic cotton and hemp. Diaper covers come in cool designs, making cloth a fashion statement. For additional information on cloth diapers and other accessories, check out www.mother-ease.com, www.clothdiaper.com, www.cottonbabies.com, and www.diaperjunction.com.

A Meditation on Strollers and Slings

There are plenty of options when it comes to carrying babies. Some people prefer using strollers to roll about town, while others prefer carrying babies up close in a sling or carrier. It's really a personal preference. Concerns with strollers are that they are made using plastic and soft polyvinyl chloride (PVC) coverings. Not only is this a concern with babies chewing on the materials; other issues also arise from the environmental impact of the manufacturing process. Although no studies specifically addressing strollers have been done, studies on toys show that babies don't chew on the toys long enough to absorb chemicals. Parents who are bothered by the idea of buying a stroller and supporting the petrochemical industry can consider purchasing a secondhand stroller. Not only are many strollers made to last multiple children; a used stroller will also be less expensive than a new model.

Slings and baby carriers come in all shapes, sizes, and patterns and allow parents to keep babies close while keeping their hands free. Some slings snuggle the baby right up to Mom or Dad's chest while others, usually those for older infants, are worn on the hips. There are also styles that are worn on the parent's back. If you are interested in looking for different designs and more information on slings and carriers, check out www.sevenbaby.com and www.mobywrap.com.

The Tao of Toys

Kids nuzzle everything, rubbing it on their faces and putting it in their mouths, so parents want to make sure their toys are as safe as can be. The Federal Hazardous Substances Act and respective amendments, along with the 1969 Child Protection and Toy Safety Act, govern safety regulations for toys sold in the United States. Regulations are enforced by the Consumer Product Safety Commission (CPSC) and include testing requirements for the following:

- Paint and other surface coatings
- Pacifiers and rattles
- Noise levels
- Electric or thermal toys
- Chemistry sets
- Sharp edges and points
- Small parts or choking hazards
- Flammability
- Hazardous substances

When it comes to toys, concern over the materials and chemicals used are furthered by the amount of manufacturing done in countries with minimal regulations. Chemicals added to plastic to soften it include phthalates, which are considered a carcinogen by the EPA. Phthalates are also suspected as endocrine disrupters that can affect hormonal activities in laboratory animals. There is concern that children could absorb phthalates contained in the toys when chewing on them; however, studies have shown that the children do not chew the toys long enough for the chemicals to be absorbed. Some countries consider the levels of phthalates allowed in US toys too high; the European Union has banned six specific phthalates.

Teaching Your Kids

Enlightening children about the environment can be just as much fun for adults as it is for kids. It gives parents a chance to learn something they may have been interested in or share some of their knowledge. There are a lot of different ways for parents to help their children appreciate the world around them. Many schools incorporate some aspect of environmental awareness in their curriculum, but parents play the most important role in leading their children toward environmental stewardship.

Experience the Outdoors

Field trips can be a great way to expose kids to the wonders of the environment firsthand. To get the most out of the excursion, the location and length of a visit should be age-appropriate. Consider taking children to a science museum, particularly one that's geared at least partially toward a child's interest. Here children are allowed to see, touch, and even crawl on or climb through nature exhibits. The Florida Museum of Natural History (www.floridamuseum.ufl.edu) on the campus of the University of Florida is home to a life-size limestone cave. Children and parents can walk through it, looking at geologic formations and searching for bats and other animals. The museum also has a screened-in butterfly rain forest that houses subtropical and tropical trees and plants that support hundreds of free-flying butterflies. Many museums also offer docents who will lead a tour, telling stories and providing information.

If you are looking for the real thing, take a trip to a park and experience nature firsthand on a nature walk looking for bugs and other wildlife. Some parks are home to rocks and formations that offer their own learning experience. Some parks regularly offer ranger-led walks, or one can be scheduled ahead of time, that will point out what the park has to offer. What better way to learn about the environment than seeing it firsthand with a professional?

Hands-on activities can really pique a child's interest. Exploring a park can lead to picking up litter and checking for animal footprints as well as discussions on recycling and protecting animal habitats.

Local farms offer another outing. Taking children out to pick local fruit can show them how food is grown and harvested. They will learn what grows in their region with respect to the seasons. Even a trip to the grocery store can be a learning experience if you point out the labels and talk about where the fruits and vegetables were grown.

Some zoos offer children's camps, where kids can be zookeepers for the day and learn about the animals, their environment, and the threats they face. Parents can also take advantage of open houses offered at local animal rehabilitation centers and veterinary schools to give children a little more insight into the environment.

Noble Reads, Green Reads

Reading to your kids can be fun and purposefully green! Books that help nurture naturalists can range from warm and fuzzy stories from authors like Eve Bunting and James Herriot to more informative nature books series such as DK Eyewitness books and Owlet Press books. Childsake offers lists of environmental and nature books for children, organizing them by category (www.childsake.com). Your local librarian may also have some suggestions.

Magazines introduce kids to environmental topics in quick gulps. *Ranger Rick*, *Kids Discover*, and *National Geographic Kids* give children the opportunity to learn about all different aspects of the natural world around them and ways to take care of it.

The Internet also offers an array of sites that teach environmental lessons. Many state and local regulatory agencies have pages expressly for children. The EPA sponsors Environmental Education at www.epa.gov. Nonprofit organizations also offer information designed for children. Audubon Adventures (www.audubonadventures.org) offers lessons for kids in kindergarten through twelfth grade that can be incorporated into classroom activities.

Healthful Snacks and Brown Bags

Snacks now come in convenient portion-controlled packages. Many teachers even request that group snacks be provided to the classroom already prepackaged and individually wrapped. Not only do single-portion packages cost a lot; they also produce an excessive amount of waste as all of the single wrappers are tossed in the trash. So while grabbing a snack out of the pantry and heading out the door may be convenient, there are more environmentally friendly alternatives.

You can buy snacks in bulk, or at least more than a single-serving container, and pack individual servings in reusable containers yourself. You can also make snacks at home and pack them in lunches or take them to the park. The same goes for drinks. There's no need to buy juice boxes or bottled water. Use washable bottles and fill them with 100 percent juice or tap water to wash down your snacks.

If you're looking for suggestions for packing a healthy lunch for younger kids, check out www.bentology.com. The website offers colorful and innovative lunchboxes and containers as well as menu support.

Many children take lunches that are completely prepackaged from drink to dessert. They produce a hefty amount of trash because nothing is reusable and much of the lunch often goes uneaten. Moreover, these lunches contain very little nutrition and a lot of fat and preservatives. When packing a child's lunch, take advantage of reusable containers and only pack what you think your child will eat. This will set a precedent so that when kids begin packing their own lunches, they'll go for the reusable containers and use portion control automatically.

Parents can also invest in plastic lunchboxes or reusable bags for their child's lunch. Reusing brown paper bags several times and then recycling them is another option.

PATIENCE, WISDOM, AND TEENS

Teenagers may take a lead role in your family's learning curve when it comes to going green. Through high school and local community programs, they're on the forefront and see conservation as their generation's greatest contribution.

Parents may also lend a hand in creating and directing opportunities for teens. Becoming involved with certain groups can help improve teenagers' self-esteem and introduce them to other teens with similar interests. Some opportunities may offer insight to future careers, while others may help students accrue volunteer hours needed for school or college. Teens can do environmental research for a science fair project. Topics can include burying waste to determine how long it takes to degrade or watering plants with acidic liquid to determine the effect of acid rain. By performing the research and the experiment, students can learn environmental lessons firsthand.

If teenagers want to experience the outdoors and learn about the environment, they can participate in a parks program. Some programs include helping maintain facilities or teaching and leading children, while others focus on adventure. Many national parks partner with NatureBridge to offer students overnight trips to explore the ecosystem. Backpacking, rafting, and rock climbing trips can be found, and some include options for campers to perform research that could lead to college credit. More information on these programs is available online at http://naturebridge.org.

Rather than sit on the sidelines listening to adults, teens can be active participants in environmental, humanitarian, and animal causes. Teens can join organizations geared toward their age group or they can mix it up with other ages. Many organizations such as the Humane Society have a special branch just for teens. The Humane Teens organization provides teens with information on starting projects that can help animals in their own town.

Holistic Healthcare

A pediatrician is an important figure when it comes to raising a child. Parents rely on the pediatrician to provide accurate answers to their questions. But medicine, like other practices, has different methods and approaches, so when you are choosing a pediatrician select one who shares your beliefs. Pediatricians should be patient in answering your questions as well as validating your concerns, and while doctors may be experts in their field, the parent-doctor relationship should be a partnership.

Like other doctors, there are pediatricians who practice holistic medicine. These doctors have received medical degrees and have continued their education with holistic coursework. Holistic doctors use conventional medicines and immunizations, but they also consider the whole child and how he or she fits in the environment. Doctors who practice holistic or complementary medicine encourage patients and families to include lifestyle as part of the healing process and encourage prevention over treatment if possible.

Many mainstream doctors are trying to decrease the amount of drugs they prescribe, especially when it comes to cases of mild depression. Studies have found that exercise or even joining a club helps alleviate symptoms. This is particularly promising when it comes to medicating children.

Complementary medical practitioners may also include positive visualization, chiropractic, and probiotics as part of their regimen. They work with parents on other alternative treatments for chronic illnesses to help alleviate the cause rather than the symptoms.

Often, there are natural and herbal remedies that can relieve a baby's discomfort, from diaper rash to colic. Ask your doctor or visit your local health food store to see what remedies they can suggest.

Another option to traditional medicine is seeking the services of a doctor of osteopathy (DO). DOs obtain educations similar to traditional medical doctors and can perform the same duties. The difference lies in their approach to medicine—much like a holistic practitioner, a DO tends to take a step back when diagnosing a problem to look at the big picture. They tend to become general care practitioners, focusing on preventive medicine and psychological and social factors relating to their patients.

CHAPTER TEN

Responsible Pet Care

Buddha says, "The way is in the heart." Humans have a
responsibility to animals, especially domesticated animals under
our care. To neglect them is to neglect our own sense of compassion
and well-being. As family pets are 100 percent dependent upon
our decisions and nurturing, our practices of self-care and safety
should be extended to them. Besides, rare are the moments
when pure love is readily available in return.

Pets are family too and can't be overlooked when it comes to safe products that enhance the life and health of your furry, finned, or feathered friends. Pets fill roles as devoted friends, surrogate children, personal assistants, and even therapists. As a pet owner, there are choices people can make to take pet ownership to a greener level and give back to their pet. This chapter offers information on ways you can choose and raise pets while helping the environment.

PAVE THE PATH FOR PETS

Domesticated animals play an important role in the lives of most people. They provide an opportunity for children and adults to learn the skills of caring, nurturing, and responsibility. Popular programs exist today in which dogs and cats are used in various healthcare environments, ushering in a gentle love that benefits those suffering from long-term illness, pain, and the sense of isolation that can accompany hospitalization. Making a fuss over pets isn't a new trend, but it is a growing, prosperous industry. Pets have been catered to for thousands of years, even having their own private servants.

Walking the dog can be an important part of a weight loss program for you and your pet, making the time outdoors more enjoyable. Picking up a leash instead of a snack is a lot more fun and beneficial. People are not the only ones benefiting from exercise; it can extend a dog's life and burn off extra energy, making them more relaxed.

Pets don't always have it so good and it's a community's responsibility—collectively—to protect them out of respect for life. Crimes against animals are unethical. The American Society for the Prevention of Cruelty to Animals (ASPCA) and the Humane

Society of the United States (HSUS) have a long history of working to protect animals. Many communities also have local rescue groups who fill the gaps between local government agencies and the streets. Such grassroots agencies are always looking for volunteers and donations of leashes (new or used) and food products.

Some groups focus on particular animals and breeds, and others focus on specific concerns such as unscrupulous breeders or farm animal rights. These local and national animal protection organizations work diligently to educate people and help alleviate animal suffering. Hurricanes and natural disasters over the last several years have brought to light issues of animal safety during mass evacuations. Recently, the Pets Evacuation and Transportation Standards (PETS) Act was signed into law, requiring states to prepare pet evacuation plans. These plans must be given to the Federal Emergency Management Agency (FEMA) before funding is received. The act also authorizes money to create pet-friendly shelters. Now those in the midst of a disaster do not have to choose between their own safety and that of their pets.

CHOOSING SMART WITH HEART

Those big brown eyes through a metal cage at the local shelter can pull your heart strings, but it's important for both you and your potential pet that you choose an animal that's right for you, your family, and your lifestyle. Consider not just how cute it is, but how it will fit into your family and home.

Rescue and adoption groups are becoming very strict on their applications for adoption. For example, an adoption application that indicates a dog will be housed primarily outside, or chained because of containment issues (no fence), is considered an issue for most, and will often be rejected. Statistics have proven, sadly, that impulse rather than intelligence often drives the purchase or adoption of too many pets. Therefore, adoption groups have stepped up their advocacy for educated partners in the process and homes that can truly provide all that an animal needs.

RESPONSIBLE POPULATION CONTROL

Spaying or neutering a pet is one of the greenest decisions you can make. There is an overpopulation of pets, both pure and mixed breeds, and millions of animals are euthanized every year. Operation Catnip humanely traps feral cats so they can be sterilized and then returns them to the wild. The organization operates with volunteers who capture and release the animals, and veterinarians who donate time and resources to perform the surgeries. They have organizations in several southern US cities and can process up to one hundred cats in a matter of hours.

There are many programs available to assist with the cost of neutering or spaying a pet and other programs spay and neuter cats that have been abandoned or are strays. Feral cats are wary of people and congregate in groups for protection and food. By releasing them back to their environment, the cats can stay together without multiplying.

PET NOURISHMENT

Owners love their pets and want to make sure they are feeding them well. Common pet foods for sale in the grocery or discount store are inexpensive and convenient to purchase; more than likely, natural pet foods require a special trip and are usually more expensive. Is there really a difference? Well, yes.

The Essence of Pet Food

The differences involve the quality of the ingredients and the degree of processing. Pet food contains protein from various sources. The protein comes primarily from the ground remains of animal processing such as the heads, feet, and intestines; it is the discards of the human food industry. This practice allows farmers to gain added revenue rather than having to pay to get rid of waste, and it provides the pet food industry with a low-cost protein supply. Preservatives are also added to pet food to ensure that it lasts for months, in the grocery store and at home. Many commercial pet foods include grains that are not digestible by dogs and cats. Even though grains contribute relatively small amounts of protein compared to meat, this is done so that the label will reflect a certain concentration of protein.

The meat processed into by-product meal or meat and bone meal may be from sick or unhealthy animals. The meat products are processed through an extruder that steams the material under high pressure to form food nuggets. This processing destroys the nutritional value, requiring manufacturers to add nutrients and minerals back into the product.

Pet owners are quickly learning about the lethal dangers of some sweet treats made for humans—not pets. A manufactured sweetener called xylitol, which is used in chewing gum, candy, and some baked goods, can be lethal for pets. It causes a sudden drop in blood sugar that can result in depression, loss of coordination, and seizures. Large doses can bring on symptoms quickly, while symptoms from smaller doses may not show up for twelve hours. Sadly, the reports keep mounting of dogs helping themselves to a container of no-sugar-added mints containing xylitol from their owner's counter or purse. The FDA is responsible for regulating the pet food industry but does not require premarket approval before a pet food can be sold. Instead, its responsibilities lie with ensuring that the ingredients are safe and necessary, and that the food is labeled correctly with the manufacturer's name and contact information along with all of the ingredients.

The Association of American Feed Control Officials (AAFCO) is made up of federal and state regulators. The group has no regulatory authority, but it is involved in developing model laws and regulations, uniform feed ingredient definitions, and appropriate labeling.

When choosing a pet food, it's important to pick a brand that has an AAFCO guarantee and cites feeding tests or feeding profiles, not just nutrient profiles. Many natural recipes will include higher quality protein without by-products. Look for labels that include identified meat like chicken, lamb, or beef as the first ingredient, not just the word *meat*. Natural pet food will most likely not use chemical preservatives but will rely on vitamins C and E to partially or fully preserve food. As an added bonus, some natural foods are sold in recycled packaging.

If you want to change your pet's diet, don't try it all at once. Although owners may prefer a change to more natural food, a sudden change may upset a healthy pet's digestive system. A small portion of the new food can be mixed with a larger portion of the old food to slowly introduce more and more of the new food. When changing pet foods, watch your companion for any warning signs, such as changes in coat, body weight, or odor, that may indicate the new food is not agreeing with them.

Creative Pet Food

One sure way to know your pets are getting a balanced and natural diet is to make their food at home. This may also prove successful if your animal companion suffers from reactions from commercial food. If planning to make homemade pet food, it's important to meet the animal's nutritional requirements. You can consult a veterinarian or a veterinary nutritionist on the appropriate breakdown of protein, vegetables, and grain and any other vitamins or minerals that need to be added. When planning your pet's meals, be sure to know what foods your pet shouldn't eat, such as milk and onions. You don't need to spend hours slaving over a dinner for your pet, either. Some animals, like dogs, can handle eating raw meat without problems. If you would like to switch your pet to a homemade diet, do it gradually, just as if you were changing pet foods.

HOLISTIC PET CARE

Just as with your own doctors, it's important to make sure you see eye to eye with your veterinarian. Some pet owners are very happy with traditional vets while others seek the extended services of a holistic practitioner. Holistic vets have degrees in traditional veterinary medicine but take additional coursework in more natural approaches to healing and helping animals.

Holistic medicine is generally used to treat chronic conditions, not traumatic injuries. Vets that use holistic methods still employ traditional approaches such as vaccinations, x-rays, and pharmaceuticals, but they also look at the whole animal and consider other treatments when healing or improving the condition of a patient, including diet and emotional well-being. Holistic vets also look at alternative medicines such as the following:

- Acupuncture
- Behavior modification
- Chiropractic therapy
- Herbal remedies
- Homeopathy
- Nutritional therapy

When it comes to other aspects of pet care such as flea control, owners should make sure they are on the same page as their vet in looking for solutions that everyone feels comfortable with.

Sacrificing Fleas

If you bring home a dog or a cat, there will have to be decisions on flea control, for everyone's sake. Fleas can irritate a pet's skin, which can result in open sores and hair loss. Battling fleas and flea bites makes life hard on pets and their owners.

Adult fleas feed on the blood of pets—and possibly on people living in the house as well. They're strong and gravity has little impact on them; they're able to jump sideways as far as 5 feet and straight up as high as 9 inches.

There are a plethora of synthetic chemicals on the market to help owners wage war on fleas. These dips, sprays, and topical ointments all contain pesticides that are absorbed into a pet's body through their skin. Fleas are able to build up a resistance to these chemicals, requiring new formulas to be produced. While these flea treatments work very well in most cases, they can pose a danger to the pet and possibly even others in the house. Potential risks with using flea treatment can be researched on the EPA website (www.epa.gov), which contains fact sheets for a variety of active ingredients.

Organic pesticides are available to control fleas. Even though they are derived naturally, they may still pose a threat and are not acceptable to some. Pyrethrin derivatives are made from chrysanthemums and are used to make dips and sprays. According to the EPA, they are the least toxic pesticide to mammals.

There was some concern that pyrethrins may cause cancer, but so far there are no data to support this idea. However, they have been shown to cause skin and breathing problems in some cases. While they do break down in nature, they are highly toxic to fish. Diatomaceous earth is fossilized algae that has turned to dust. Used in powder form, the sharp edges of the fine particles cut into the flea's exoskeleton, causing them to dehydrate and die. Because of the fine particles, take care to minimize the dust both people and pets breathe in. This powder can be used directly on the pet, as well as on bedding and furniture.

You can set flea traps by placing a soapy dish of water under a light. The fleas will be attracted to the warmth and will drown in the soapy water. Also, when combing out pets, keep a cup of soapy water handy. Pull fleas off the comb and drop them into the water; the soap makes it difficult or impossible for the fleas to escape, leaving the tiny biters in a watery grave.

Flea shampoos can be especially harmful to young kittens and puppies. Rescue workers who foster young kittens and puppies—often dropped by the roadside and rescued in flea-ridden, poor health—have found Dawn dish soap to be a great, effective alternative. Dawn (the original, not the newer herbal varieties) does a good job of both safely cleaning the animal and washing away flea debris, while also acting as a disinfectant/antibacterial without harmful side effects. It may take a couple of wash/rinse rounds, but does an overall great job in a safe manner.

There are shampoos made specifically for adult pets, but using a mild or baby shampoo on your pet may work just as well as fancy products marketed as just for pets. Adult dogs prone to dry eye do well with diluted baby shampoos designed to be less irritating on the eyes.

Consult with your veterinarian or groomer; they'll know best. In any case, your pet does not need to bathe nearly as often as you do. Washing your pet too frequently will dry its skin, resulting in an itchy and miserable companion.

Organic shampoos and skin treatments are available that use organic, biodegradable ingredients. The popularity of the green movement along with the need to pamper pets has led to a market for organic grooming products.

CHAPTER ELEVEN

Buying or Building with Awareness

A home is much more than a structure to provide shelter.
It's an extension of your personality and preferences, your creativity and
utility, and, in terms of Zen, a statement of your health and happiness.
Using renewable resources when building or renovating a home shows
right action, and offers you comfort, stability, and energy efficiency
while supporting the well-being of Earth.

Starting over, whether you're considering buying a new home or building one, offers a unique opportunity to consider green; a greener community, green materials for remodeling, and cost-effective new building practices that lend themselves to natural products.

With a public upsurge in environmental concerns, many cities and states have taken the initiative to make improvements and make themselves a haven for environmentally friendly citizens. If you know where you are going to live, you can choose to use more environmentally friendly home designs and construction materials. This chapter outlines the ways and means to find a green city or build a green house.

THE EMERALD CITY-STATE

Many mayors are taking it upon themselves to be good stewards of the environment. They are taking actions to improve air quality, reduce electrical use and production, encourage eco-friendly building construction, allocate more green space, support nontraditional transportation, and set aside or improve areas for recreational activities.

The United States Conference of Mayors is just one coalition working to improve cities in a variety of ways. In an effort to improve air quality, 1,066 mayors have pledged accordance with the Mayors Climate Protection Agreement, a pact that encourages each city to reduce greenhouse gas emissions below 1990 levels. The organization shares ideas and outcomes from programs they have implemented, providing a network of environmental actions and results for others to learn from. This is just one example of how communities are working together to improve conditions in their own cities and towns.

When it comes to good stewardship, Austin, Texas; San Francisco; Portland, Oregon; Boston; Honolulu; and many others have been identified by sites like www.directenergy.com as showing success. Chicago and Minneapolis are very conscientious when it comes to encouraging clean air and water, promoting green building, and ensuring that parks and open spaces are protected. Portland, Oregon, got the top spot Direct Energy blog's list for 2018 because of its numerous bike trails, open space, and commitment to renewable resources. Forty-nine percent of the city's power is provided by hydroelectricity and wind power. Portland has set a goal of reaching 100 percent renewable energy by 2050.

States may not be involved on the same level as cities, but they still take measures to make themselves more environmentally friendly to homeowners. States on both coasts have come together to reduce greenhouse gas emissions. The West Coast Governors' Global Warming Initiative, including California, Oregon, and Washington, puts limits on greenhouse gas emissions and commits the states to using increasing amounts of renewable energy. In fact, if California, Oregon, and Washington were a country, they would rank seventh in the world in terms of the least greenhouse gas emissions. California alone would rank twelfth.

Nine states on the other side of the country—Connecticut, Delaware, Maine, Massachusetts, New Hampshire, New Jersey, New York, Rhode Island, and Vermont—formed the Regional Greenhouse Gas Initiative with similar aims to reduce greenhouse gas emissions.

Federal and state tax incentives or local utility rebates may be available for energy-efficient products purchased and installed in your home. The cost of Energy Star–rated appliances like solar water heaters, photovoltaic cells, and windows can sometimes be deducted from federal income tax. The North Carolina Solar Center publishes a list of state incentives and programs. The state-by-state list is available on www.dsireusa.org.

Today, 90 percent of new homes built in the United States are Energy Star compliant. The EPA and the Department of Energy created Energy Star criteria to give homeowners and contractors guidelines and direction when looking for more sustainable approaches to construction. Energy Star rates homes, businesses, and household products for energy efficiency. The Energy Star website, www.energystar.gov, has more information.

Finding Your Own Nirvana

If you are looking for a clean start in a new city, there are a few telltale signs to consider when it comes to making a choice. If environmental stewardship, recreational opportunities, or mass transit systems figured into your decision, tell the community by writing to the mayor's office and local newspapers. If more cities see these factors as magnets drawing people to them, it will reinforce the connection between environmental quality and economic viability.

Air quality is an important consideration when it comes to calling a place home. How does a city rank for fuel exhaust pollution? The EPA maintains an Air Quality Index (www.airnow.gov) that scores ozone and particulate matter for different cities across the United States.

Another link to air quality is a city's ability to encourage environmentally friendly transportation. Mass transit systems cut down on the number of personal vehicles on the road, reduce parking and congestion problems, and limit or decrease greenhouse gas emissions and smog. Conscientious cities also provide carpool lanes, dedicated bicycle lanes, walking trails, and sidewalks and are designed to run efficiently without the need for individually owned vehicles.

The sources of a city's energy correlate not just to the degradation of air quality, but to the generation of greenhouse gases as well. If you want to live in a city that's going beyond the norm when it comes to energy generation, look for cities that either already use or are making headway with alternative fuels such as biomass, geothermal, hydroelectric, solar, and wind. Websites with information on cities that use alternative fuels include www.sustainlane.us and www.energy.gov/eere/office-energy-efficiency-renewable-energy.

City designers that take into account not just buildings but green space understand an important aspect of improving environmental quality. Eco-friendly spaces provided by a municipality include athletic fields and parks as well as walking and biking trails along with recreational water and clean water resources. The US Green Building Council (USGBC) runs the Leadership in Energy and Environmental Design (LEED) program, setting criteria for what is considered a green building. LEED takes into account human and environmental health, sustainable site development, water savings, energy efficiency, material selection, and indoor environmental quality. Some builders specifically design houses or developments with sustainability in mind. When looking for a house, find out if the community includes any of these developments. Also, if you're looking for a builder familiar with green construction, visit www.energystar.gov, where builders familiar with environmentally friendly home construction are listed by city and state.

Municipal recycling programs are also one indication of a city's dedication to the environment. Recycling not only conserves natural resources; it also reduces the energy needed to make recycled products. If you're moving, you can consider choosing a city that encourages recycling with curbside programs and recycling centers that go beyond the standard glass, paper, and aluminum. When performed well, recycling programs not only offset the cost of waste disposal; they can also generate income for an area. Recycling can be a sophisticated business; running a successful operation means keeping up with current trends, technology, and other professionals. There are challenges to recycling, however, such as when the energy required to transport the reclaimed materials offsets any potential gains.

Portland, Oregon, puts an emphasis on being sustainable. It was the first US city to implement a plan to reduce carbon dioxide emissions. Oregon relies on hydroelectric power for 44 percent of its energy production. Portland recycles not only the standard glass, metal, and plastic but also accepts residential yard waste and food from businesses for compost. Feeling safe about the water delivered from the tap is something to consider too. The EPA requires that municipalities' water quality be documented and reported as part of the Safe Drinking Water Act. The EPA does not maintain the data in a searchable format, but it can direct any interested party to information on a particular water system. Towns, cities, and utilities should have this information on hand and may even post it on their website. Safe drinking water should not contain compounds that are required to be monitored at levels exceeding the EPA Drinking Water Standards. Data that are available for review should note any levels in excess of allowable concentrations.

Finding a Sacred Area in Any Town

If you already know what town or city you are going to live in, either due to family, work, or environmental reasons, there are still choices about which part of town to live in. Consider all of your commutes—to work, school, the grocery store, and other regular activities. Take into account the frequency of those trips and when they'll be made. What appears to be a great location at two in the afternoon may turn ugly during rush hour. If you are relocating, start looking at places that will give you the shortest trip miles through the week. This strategy will save money that you would spend on fuel and reduce wear and tear on the car, and it may also offer the possibility of biking or walking to some destinations.

What are the mass transit routes and other transportation opportunities for work or school? Is carpooling an option? Or is a subway or train station located nearby? An activity that a family member participates in regularly may also be a controlling consideration. Weigh all the factors.

Although debated by many, urban sprawl is blamed for many of society's woes. Urban sprawl indeed fragments and destroys wildlife habitat and corridors. The persistent construction of low-density housing developments requires additional roads and cars to navigate them, altering natural water runoff pathways and contributing to petroleum by-products that wash into the sewer system. Unless houses or developments are constructed to be independent from municipal services, other infrastructure systems such as water, wastewater, and electricity have to be expanded to accommodate spreading cities.

KARMIC DESIGN

Mother Nature should be your ultimate general contractor, helping with heating and cooling. In locations with warm climates, the broad side of the house should face north or south to avoid a direct hit—and resulting heat gain—from the sun. Deep overhangs will also help block the sun and reduce excessive heat gains by putting the house in the shade. Tint can be applied to windows, particularly sliding glass doors or large picture windows that can heat up a room quickly and force an air conditioner to work overtime. Without impacting the view, tinting can provide a savings of 5 to 10 percent of the energy needed to cool a house when applied to western-facing windows. Windows facing east also let heat into a house; however, because houses are usually not as hot in the morning when the sun is rising, savings may not be as great. In colder climates, take advantage of the sun's heating abilities. Heat provided from the sun can be stored in the concrete or stone walls of a house, helping to keep it warm even after the sun goes down.

Solar screens reduce heat and glare from the sun but allow the light to enter the house without impeding the outside view. Trees can provide natural solar protection. Some trees are particularly useful in blocking the sun because of their height and shape. It's important to choose a tree that is native to the location for optimal health and lower maintenance. If it's an option, retain as many of the existing trees as possible when building on a new lot. They'll provide shade and have already proven themselves as being viable on the property.

When it comes to building a green house, make sure to do your homework. There are sources available online (e.g., www.energystar.gov) and at your local bookstore with information on green building alternatives and designs. Look for contractors and designers with experience in sustainability and find out what other houses they have built. Ask for referrals and then give their clients a call.

Soil can also be an essential source for maintaining the temperature of a home. By building a home partially below grade, you can maintain a more moderate temperature year-round. The earth is usually cooler than above ground, so heating may be necessary to maintain a comfortable temperature in cold weather. However, because the soil provides insulation, the heat will remain in the house rather than escape to the outside. Energy-conscious contractors and architects will work with you to achieve your goals. Many of the same new construction considerations apply to renovation. You should be able to discuss alternatives with your contractor to ensure that sustainable elements are brought into the design. Also, if you are demolishing older portions of a home, the material being removed should be reclaimed and reused or handled properly to avoid excessive waste.

If your contractor is not familiar with recycling programs in the area, it may be worthwhile for you to make some phone calls. Habitat for Humanity, a nonprofit organization that builds homes, runs a program called ReStore that accepts donations of used or excess building materials in good condition. Local solid-waste authorities may also have information on specific recyclers in the area. Try calling salvage companies to see what kind of material they are interested in.

Buddha's Building Materials

Choosing building materials to preserve natural resources means using elements from renewable resources that help conserve energy and improve the health and well-being of those inside. Qualities to look for in these materials include conserving resources, improving indoor air quality, being energy efficient, and conserving water. Most important, make sure the materials are affordable not just for construction, but also to operate on a month-by-month basis.

Recyclables

From the outside in, there are a variety of recycled materials available for building homes. Products made from recycled materials require less energy to produce and use ingredients that would otherwise need to be disposed of in a landfill or incinerator. Starting from the bottom up, the foundation of most homes can be made using concrete that incorporates fly ash (the remnants from coal power plants) and even recycled concrete. Depending on the construction, it could be possible to incorporate the foundation into the finished floor design, which would require fewer building materials than usual.

Buying Recycled Products

If you are shopping for construction materials, look for products with the recycled symbol: three arrows chasing each other in the shape of a triangle. If you are working with a contractor, discuss up-front the need to use recycled materials. Many recycled construction materials are available, including roof material, gypsum board, steel studs, siding, and fascia. Because of customer demand, larger home-improvement stores are beginning to stock more recycled building products.

Recycled paper is being employed in a variety of different home projects. For example, a mixture of cement and paper, called papercrete, is being used to make bricks for home construction. The blocks are strong and provide excellent insulation from weather and sound. A variety of mixes can be used with lesser or greater amounts of cement, depending on your personal preference and the desired end result.

Concrete isn't without its environmental flaws. It requires the mining of materials, such as limestone, which alters the land and surface-water flow and affects inhabitants of nearby areas. Its production is energy intensive, not just in mining and transport but in processing as well; this energy is usually produced by coal-fired power plants. Carbon dioxide is produced by the power plants used to supply electricity to the processing facility and as part of the chemical process of converting limestone into lime. The process also produces sulfur dioxide and nitrous oxides. Particulate matter, or dust, is also created during the mining, storage, and transportation of the materials. Although the mining and processing associated with making concrete has improved over the decades, there are still issues that make reducing the amount produced practical.

Using papercrete reduces the need to purchase and produce cement. The bricks made from papercrete can be used to build straight walls, providing a finished product that looks similar to most standard homes. Papercrete can also be used to construct arches and domes. When constructing domes, the need for roofing materials is eliminated, another positive attribute to using this building material.

Cellulose, or recycled paper, can also be used in making fiberboard and gypsum-board sheeting material. Cellulose is used for the interior walls of homes. Recycled paper can be incorporated into insulation. The liquid pulp can be blown into walls or attics, offering an alternative to fiberglass insulation. High-density polyethylene (HDPE), which comes from used milk jugs, juice bottles, and detergent containers, can be recycled into lumber substitutes. This material is generally not used for indoor construction, but it is becoming more and more popular for outdoor decking and fencing. It's a common component of outdoor amenities such as benches, picnic tables, and trash cans. Not only does HDPE use recycled materials—it also avoids the need to use lumber that needs to be treated to withstand weather and insects.

Renewable Materials

Materials that are grown to be harvested, such as bamboo, are preferable to those whose supply is limited for use in homebuilding and repairs. Examples of renewable materials include wood from forests that are harvested using sustainable methods. These resources are managed so that there is as little impact on the environment as possible. Sustainable products also provide resources and incomes to local populations where they are harvested.

Companies offering renewable resources ensure limited use of chemicals, provide conservation zones, and provide protection for rare or threatened species. By growing resources, farmers can properly use the land while providing for their families and villages without damaging the environment and hindering its future use.

The Zen of Salvaging

Interior fixtures can be reused just like external building materials. Salvaging or reusing materials has many advantages. Some people who could not afford antiques inherit vintage material such as beautifully grained wood flooring or heavy steel door handles. By looking to demolition sites, builders can obtain materials that would otherwise have been disposed of, and allow them to live on in someone else's home. When reusing older building materials, for example, plumbing and lighting fixtures should be checked to ensure they meet current building codes before they're installed. When designing a new home or remodeling an existing one, homeowners can contact local salvage companies to see what is available. Many carry an evolving and changing stock of cast-iron bathtubs, oak mantels, and stained-glass windows. Contractors working as salvage companies used to be rare entities, but they are becoming more common. The relationship works best if customers can be patient and wait for just the right piece.

Dumpster diving is more than recycling; it's a social network. In communities all over the country, dumpster divers meet up online and in person to share stories and tips. Before you go diving in, check your local laws to avoid being cited for trespassing. Divers should never leave a mess; it is not environmentally friendly and will give other divers, or recyclers, a bad name.

Pondering the Larger Picture

When selecting new materials for building a home, be sure to consider how and where items were made. Does the manufacturer have environmentally sound principles? Do they use recycled materials?

Do they recycle their postindustrial materials? Using locally produced materials eliminates the waste created by transporting the items long distances. This not only reduces the need to use fossil fuels—it also reduces the impacts of manufacturing and using petroleum products.

ZEN YOUR ENERGY

Harnessing power from nature and reducing energy usage may make it possible to get off the power grid. From solar to wind and other alternatives, there is a variety of renewable energy options available for keeping lights bright, food cold, and temperature just right whether your home is on or off the power grid.

Contemplating the Grid

One of the aspects of supplying your own power is how the system will be connected to the grid or electrical network. The national power grid is a network of transmission and distribution systems owned by public companies or investor-owned utilities and cooperatives. Utilities and cooperatives buy and sell power to each other depending on the demand and availability. The network tries to provide redundancy; that means, if there is a problem somewhere in the grid, operations can be rerouted and service can be more easily restored.

If you are generating your own electricity through alternate means, working with your local power company may give you the option of selling excess energy you may produce. You will need to track your electricity usage; your local power provider can tell you what kind of meter you need to install. Another alternative is to bank excess power. Rather than giving excess power back to the utility, the homeowner uses it to charge batteries. When the home system is unable to generate electricity, the power stored in the batteries can be accessed.

These options allow homeowners to operate independently from the grid when generating their own power. When the grid is down, a home system may continue to operate.

Solar Power

When it comes to producing energy for your home, solar power is a great alternative. Solar energy is produced when the sun shines on photovoltaic (PV) panels. These panels hold semiconductors that use the sunlight to generate electricity in the form of direct current (DC) electricity.

Panels are usually mounted on the roof, on steel poles, or on the ground. Local regulations or neighborhood covenants may dictate the location of solar panels. Mounting the panels on the roof requires using the proper supports. It may be necessary to reinforce the roof support to maintain safety and to be in compliance with local building codes.

The National Renewable Energy Laboratory has information for homeowners on renewable alternatives. Readers can check out *A Consumer's Guide: Get Your Power from the Sun* at www.nrel.gov/docs/fy04osti/35297.pdf.

Wind Power

While most suburban neighborhoods won't allow the space necessary, depending on where you live, wind can provide the means of powering your house. Maps indicating wind energy potential are available to determine whether homes you are considering are located within an area where wind power would be an effective method of providing power. The website www.energy.gov/eere/ office-energy-efficiency-renewable-energy lists wind conditions by state, allowing homeowners in the US to determine if wind power is a suitable alternative for generating their own energy.

Heating and Cooling

What we need most can often be equally confusing. The EPA rates heating and cooling systems using the Energy Star logo to symbolize systems that are more efficient and use less energy, and most utility companies will reward your choice by means of a rebate check. Usually these systems are quieter and have longer lives, reducing equipment waste. Equipment eligible to receive the Energy Star symbol includes boilers, furnaces, heat pumps, programmable thermostats, and air conditioners.

The US Department of Energy reports that approximately 45 percent of the average utility bill goes to heating and cooling a home. Heating and cooling dwellings in the United States is responsible for producing 150 million tons of carbon dioxide annually.

Selecting the correct size system for your weather extremes and living space and choosing an efficient model are crucial ways to save energy. Frequently cleaning filters, checking ducts for leaks, and installing programmable thermostats to adjust the times the house is heated and cooled throughout the day will save on equipment wear and tear, and also on fuel costs. Installing a whole-house fan that pulls cool air in and releases warm air through the attic is another effective measure.

CHAPTER TWELVE

Decorating Beautifully and Resourcefully

In the world of Zen, using the ancient practice of feng shui to organize your home allows a flow of positive energy to circulate throughout your space—creating a balanced and harmonious place to live, meditate, and learn while on your search for Nirvana.

With the increase in environmental awareness, there are options galore when it comes to filling a home with Earth-friendly flooring, furniture, appliances, and lighting. Taking the environment into account won't just help the planet; it can save money through lower electric bills and tax incentives. This chapter gives some insight into how to conserve energy and choose home furnishings with the environment in mind. Making a home green on the inside may just save some green ($) too.

CONSERVE ENERGY, IMPROVE KARMA

The Energy Star label indicates that an appliance or electronic equipment meets certain criteria for being energy efficient. The certification means that the appliances were rated objectively, and the appliance label itself includes information on the cost savings. The symbol was introduced by the EPA in 1992 to provide consumers with information to help them choose appliances and electronics that are more efficient and produce fewer greenhouse gases than their traditional counterparts. What started with just a few pieces of equipment grew, and by 1995 the labeling was expanded to include other office equipment and residential heating and cooling equipment. In 1996, the Department of Energy (DOE) jumped onboard and began working with the EPA. The label now appears on more than thirty-five different kinds of products.

Energy Star Appliances

When considering kitchen appliances, look for the Energy Star symbol. While the initial cost of the appliance may be higher than those without the star symbol, energy savings throughout the life of the appliance will more than cover the additional purchase expense. If you take into account the initial purchase price, maintenance costs, and operational costs for a large appliance, you can expect to save about $200 a year; extending that amount over an expected operating life of five to ten years results in considerable savings. In addition to saving you money, buying Energy Star appliances will also help you walk the path of green living. Most appliances use water and electricity or natural gas, so buying energy-efficient models conserves all three.

The Turn-Off

Electronics and appliances can still drain energy when they are turned off. The EPA estimates that the 100 million households in the United States produce approximately 17 percent of the nation's greenhouse gases. On average, 40 percent of residential electricity goes to electronic products that are switched off, according to Energy Star. One easy way to eliminate this waste is to unplug electronics when you aren't using them.

Energy Star Homes

When energy savings are achieved throughout the house, the entire building can qualify for the Energy Star label. The EPA has published guidelines for a variety of different types of homes, including single-family and multifamily (duplexes and apartments) units;

even modular or log homes can qualify. The EPA lists the criteria needed to achieve Energy Star status, such as effective insulation, high-performance windows, tight construction and ducts, efficient heating and cooling equipment, and the use of Energy Star lighting and appliances. In order to complete the certification process, a licensed third party must verify that these standards have been met. The construction of Energy Star homes or the remodeling of older homes to meet Energy Star guidelines has increased as more contractors become familiar with the objectives. Owners of Energy Star homes know they are helping conserve natural resources by using less electricity and producing less carbon dioxide.

Positive Energy

Energy audits are a great place to begin to learn how energy efficient your home is; audits can be performed by private companies, electric utilities, or online with homeowners entering household information. A good audit will provide a homeowner with a detailed plan for possible improvements, cost estimates for those improvements, and savings estimates for the improvements over time. Some local utilities offer rebates and incentives for making energy-efficient improvements. It may be necessary to include an official audit with the rebate paperwork.

ILLUMINATING THE COSTS

As much as 15 percent of a home's electric bill is spent on lighting. Incandescent light bulbs waste upward of 95 percent of the energy as heat, making the lights only about 5 percent efficient. That's right—the main reason to flip the switch is light, but really what is being generated is heat. Because of this, incandescent bulbs can increase your need for air conditioning in the summer months, raising your electric bill and your carbon footprint. Halogen lights do not fare much better at only 9 percent efficiency.

At 20 percent efficiency, compact fluorescent lights (CFLs) are four times more efficient than incandescent lights. If your home is already equipped with incandescent lighting, rather than unscrewing the bulbs and tossing them, simply replace the five lights most frequently used. These lights are most likely in the kitchen, dining room, living room, over the bathroom vanity, and on the front porch.

By replacing just five incandescent lights with compact fluorescent lights, a standard household can save up to $60 per year. That may not sound like much, but when multiplied by all the households in the United States, the grand total is $6.5 billion a year. The pollution equivalent is that this change to CFLs would offset the same amount of greenhouse gases as eight million cars.

CFLs are a little more expensive than incandescent bulbs, but they make up for it in longevity and reduced energy use. Over the span of ten thousand hours, a CFL can cost less than half of an incandescent. In the past CFLs often flickered, but improvements have been made to stop the blinking. New models offer more variety, such as accommodating a dimmer switch. Advances in color technology have also made them more acceptable in household environments.

CFLs are more efficient because they can operate at a lower wattage. An incandescent light of 40 watts is comparable to a CFL of 14 watts. In addition, when buying CFLs, consider choosing bulbs with a color-rendering index of 80; this will make colors in your home look more natural than bulbs with lower indexes. You can check the label on the package to ensure you're making the best selection. Here are a few other energy-saving lighting tips:

- Avoid opaque light shades which require a stronger bulb.
- Lighter paints and flooring reflect light well.
- Clean dust from fixtures so their light will shine through.
- When reading or performing another task requiring focused lighting, turn off background lights and rely on a small focused lamp instead.

GROUNDED THROUGH FLOORING

Flooring options range from tile to wood, from cork to concrete, from linoleum to laminates—and then, of course, there's carpet. For allergy sufferers, non-carpet options allow easy cleaning and removal of dust and other allergens. Older flooring options had little to do with environmental impact and more with aesthetics, but that approach has changed. When picking flooring options, people often consider both their health and the environment.

Wood

Wood flooring first came on the scene during the baroque period, around the late 1600s. By the late 1800s and early 1900s, mass production and Victorian standards made wood the norm for flooring. Over the years, its popularity has waxed and waned. Today, wood is again a popular flooring alternative.

Wood flooring generally comes from domestic, exotic, or nondomestic forests. Wood flooring can also be remilled from other wood products and older flooring. Domestic flooring does not require the extensive shipping of exotics. Although hardwood flooring is a renewable resource, you need to be aware of the source of the wood you are considering. Exotic wood is sometimes harvested from forests where conditions of the local ecology and population are not taken into account. This is especially true when low prices and competition encourage irresponsible harvesting. Look for the Forest Stewardship Council (FSC) stamp of approval on wood and let it be a determining factor in your selection. The FSC is an international organization that works to promote responsible stewardship of Earth's forests by bringing together timber users, local foresters, and human rights and environmental organizations. Members include groups such as IKEA and Greenpeace. Another option in wood is salvaged wood building material; companies sell salvaged wood and cut it to specifications. Some salvagers have historical information on where the wood was recovered.

The laying and sealing of wood flooring requires the application of glues and other materials that contain volatile organic compounds or formaldehyde. These compounds can be released, causing headaches, allergic reactions, or other health problems. Look for adhesives and sealants that contain non-urea-formaldehyde.

Laminate

Laminate, which mimics the traditional wood floor, has become a popular option. It provides the same benefits as wood floor, with a reduction in sealants and the potential for better harvesting practices. Many more styles are available than when compared to its introduction in 1994.

Laminate floors are easier to install than wood floors, and many projects can be done by homeowners over a long weekend. Floating-type flooring offers planks with tongue-and-groove construction, making the planks easier to lock in place over the existing subfloor. There are some designs, however, that do require the use of glue. Laminate floors are also durable and easy to maintain. Most laminates contain wood that may or may not have been responsibly harvested. The FSC has certified some types of laminates. Other environmental concerns include off-gassing of volatile organics and formaldehyde. These chemicals are used in the manufacturing of laminates and can be released after installation is completed. Because laminate does not contain preservatives or solvents, it is unlikely to spur allergic or asthmatic reactions.

Tile and Stone

Like other noncarpet alternatives, tile and stone offer the same low-allergen amenities. Their smooth surface is not conducive to a thriving dust mite population and can be cleaned easily. Stone and tile can also last decades, meaning that manufacturing resources are conserved.

Depending on the sources of the tile and stone, there can be environmental impacts, however. The EPA requires mines to implement best management practices to avoid affecting storm water and surface water in the area. Mine reclamation, or repairing the damage to mined lands, is more common now. In addition, depending on how far they are shipped, tile and stone can weigh heavily in terms of the impacts from transportation.

Tile is often made from clay mined throughout the United States. The industry is heavily tied to construction and renovation since the clay is used mainly to make clay floor tiles. The demand for decorative floor tiles has grown, resulting in more sophisticated automation processes within the industry. Stone flooring comes in a variety of shapes and sizes. From pebbles to large slabs, stone flooring offers consumers a choice of numerous patterns and colors. Stone used in flooring is usually made of porcelain, limestone, marble, or granite, along with many others. It is installed using relatively benign mortar and grout.

Cleaning ceramic tile floors doesn't have to rely on harmful chemicals. A mixture of $\frac{1}{4}$ cup of vinegar with 1 gallon of water can be used with a terry towel to clean up a tile floor. Spills should be wiped up immediately to avoid staining the grout. If the grout does become stained, a mixture of half hydrogen peroxide and half water can be sprayed on the grout and left to sit for ten minutes. Many tile manufacturers use recycled tiles, glass, and even carpet or plastic fibers in their feedstock. Clear, brown, and green glass can be recycled and used to produce solid color and decoratively designed tiles. As with wood, laminates are now made that mimic stone and tile flooring. Also, like wood laminate, some of these floorings are produced with tongue-and-groove edges and can be installed to float above the existing floor.

Carpet

In the 1960s, carpet manufacturing technology improved, and mills moved to the South where cheap labor could mass-produce the flooring. That move started the heyday of wall-to-wall carpet. Before long, shag was the rage, and then smaller loop and cut piles moved in. While carpet provides more padding and is softer to walk and sit on, it also harbors dirt, dust mites, and other allergens like mold. There is also concern that carpets emit volatile organics and collect pesticides that are used along with other indoor contaminants. To protect your lungs, leave the house while carpet is being installed. Following installation with proper ventilation will make less of an impact on the lungs.

As other products have included recycled material in their feedstock, so has carpet. Some manufacturers rely solely on recycled plastics to produce flooring. Several different brands are made from recycled soda bottles. Because this production relies on postconsumer material, it avoids disposal of waste products in landfills and incinerators. When choosing flooring options, you may be surprised how many recycled products are available.

Authentic Alternatives

Relatively new to the flooring world are sustainable cork and bamboo. Cork flooring can be installed in much the same way as laminate and can be manufactured in a variety of colors and appearances, along with a natural cork appearance. It can even be made to look like stone or tile. With different colors available, flooring can be laid in complex or simple designs. An important feature to some is the cork's honeycomb design, which allows it to give slightly and makes it easier on the feet. This is particularly important to those who stand or cook quite a bit. The same honeycomb texture that provides comfort also absorbs noise.

Cork is harvested from the bark of cork oak trees. Trees must be twenty-five to thirty years old before they can be harvested. They are not harmed in the harvesting process. The cork will grow back and be ready for harvesting again in about ten years. Half of the cork harvested for flooring comes from Portugal.

Because cork is giving and flexible, it can be installed on floors that aren't completely level, making it particularly useful in older homes where portions of the floor may have already settled. When choosing cork flooring, check to see that it's formaldehyde-free and that any varnish is water-based.

Bamboo is actually a grass and grows fast like a weed. It's hearty and can grow in excess of 1 foot per day in poor-quality soil that is unsuitable for other crops. Known for its durability, bamboo can be harvested in as short a time as three years. The majority of bamboo is grown in China and India; but the environmental impacts from shipping can offset the benefits of using this type of flooring. When manufactured for durable flooring, bamboo maintains the appearance of hardwood but can be tinted different colors. Because it is wood, bamboo requires sealants and protective waxes. Shoppers and installers can check to see that sealants and waxes with little or no volatile organic compounds are used.

Bedding

One of the biggest environmental issues when it comes to bedding has to do with the chemicals included with the mattresses. Because so many people died of smoke inhalation and fire as a result of falling asleep while smoking in bed, the government began requiring mattresses to meet cigarette-ignition testing requirements in 1973.

Flame-retardant chemicals approved by the Consumer Product Safety Commission (CPSC) are of concern to many. Compounds include polybrominated diphenyl ethers (PBDEs). The National Institute of Environmental Health Sciences (NIEHS) voiced concern about PBDEs as their prevalence in flame-retardant materials and their persistence in the environment rose. Studies performed in Sweden indicated that PBDEs were even present in the breastmilk of nursing mothers. They have also accumulated in fish and other animals. PBDEs bioaccumulate, and tests indicate that concentrations are rising in humans, most predominantly in North America. These chemicals are suspected of causing liver and neurodevelopment toxicity.

The CPSC sponsored tests on other flame-retardant chemicals (not PBDEs) and found them to be safe either because a risk analysis showed no discernable effects or because concentrations of the chemicals were not detected in mattresses. The CPSC and other organizations, such as the Sleep Products Safety Council and the International Sleep Products Association, have stated that mattresses treated with flame retardants provide more safety from fire than risk from chemical exposure.

If you want to avoid flame retardant chemicals all together, consider a wool mattress. Wool is a natural flame retardant and can be marketed without the addition of flame retardants. Organic cotton mattresses are also sold without added chemicals, but they lack natural flame-resistant ability and can only be purchased with the written consent of a doctor.

The Water Element

Believe it or not, there are several ways to conserve natural resources and money in the bathroom. From the sink to the shower to the toilet, you can make positive environmental decisions every day.

Enlightened Elimination

Along with improvements to other appliances, great strides have been made when it comes to manufacturing more water-conserving toilets. It is estimated that about one-quarter of the water used in an average home goes to flushing the toilet if efficient toilets aren't installed. Homes built before 1992 that haven't had any improvements made are likely to have old-fashioned 3.6 gallons per flush (gpf) model toilets. Newer models use only 1.5 gallons for the same flush, and the future may hold even more efficient flushers. Not only does this reduce the amount of water being pumped from aquifers and streams, treated, and piped to the house—it also saves on treating and discharging the used water.

Another version of an efficient commode is the composting toilet. These toilets are used mainly in remote locations like weekend getaways and vacation cabins where there is no access to a sanitary sewer and septic systems aren't feasible. Compost toilets are comprised of three components: a seat, a composting chamber, and a drying tray. Some models combine all three components into one enclosure, while other designs have a separate seat. The toilets use bacteria and fungi to decompose waste, turning it into dry, fluffy humus. Regulations vary across the country; in some places, the humus can be used as fertilizer around trees and nonedible plants, but in others it must be buried or disposed of as sewage. These toilets are not supposed to smell, so if one does, chances are there's something wrong. Composting toilets do not need water, so owners reduce their household water usage and production of wastewater.

Showers and Sinks

Beyond taking shorter and colder showers, there are other steps you can take when it comes to conserving water and natural resources while cleaning up. Standard showerheads put out up to 5 gallons per minute (gpm). Low-flow showerheads can cut that in half. If a low-flow shower isn't satisfactory, try using an aerator showerhead. Air is added to the water as it flows from the head, making it feel like a higher flowing showerhead. Aerators can be added to spigots, reducing a flow of over two gpm to about one gpm. Aerators are relatively inexpensive and easy to install.

Furniture Flow

The decision to incorporate environmental furniture into a house may be driven by a desire to reduce toxins and improve indoor air quality, to promote recycling, or even to save an old-growth forest and encourage more sustainable wood harvesting.

Run-of-the-mill stuffed furniture, much like mattresses, contains fire-retardant chemicals and formaldehyde. Although regulators have said that the protection afforded by the retardants ranks higher than the potential risk of chemical health problems, you may opt to purchase less chemically protected furniture.

If you are looking to add a bit of flair to your house, check out recycled art such as bicycle sprockets made into clocks and used street signs formed into wall hangings. If your budget can't afford an artisan's work, consider making your own recycled art project. Wood furniture should have the FSC seal to ensure that it was forested with the environment and indigenous cultures in mind. Other companies now collect old wood, salvaging it from demolition sites and reworking it to make new wood furniture of both contemporary and more nostalgic styles. One example is Furniture From The Barn (https://furniturefromthebarn.com/), where customers can select hutches, benches, and dining room tables and chairs made from reclaimed lumber.

Bamboo is making headway in furniture construction too. With its strength and short harvesting time, it's a realistic alternative to traditional wood furniture. Imagine lounging in a bamboo-frame chaise atop organic cotton cushions—sustainable Nirvana.

Recycled plastic is the feedstock for some furniture designers and manufacturers. It's made mostly into patio furnishings, but some of the designs are worthy of inside rooms. Take your time when choosing any new furnishings. By checking out purchases ahead of time, you can protect the environment while investing wisely in your house.

CHAPTER THIRTEEN

Walking the Path at Work

Enlightenment can be found in unexpected places, including where you work. Duty, or commitment to your job, is a principal of Zen and duty combined with consciousness is also very green. Consider the number of hours spent at your office and all the products and services you encounter each and every day. Reducing your carbon footprint and following the wisdom of Zen at the workplace will help you on your path to peace.

By having an eco-friendly image, your business can save money while greatly assisting the environment and offering a great opportunity to stand out from the crowd in your industry or profession. Don't forget how important cause marketing is today in the world of promotion. Go ahead; toot your green horn!

You can make the service you provide or the product you make more sustainable. If you are constructing a new building or renovating an older one, look at the Green Building Council's (GBC) Leadership in Energy and Environmental Design (LEED) rating system. Your project may be certified in at least one of five areas, allowing building owners to display their certification and possibly receive incentives. If you manufacture a product, consider revising operations to meet the criteria for fair or organic trade.

EMPLOYEE-GENERATED CHANGE

The foundation of any company is built by the employees who help maintain it. Employee buy-in is key to transforming your place of business and the products you create or services rendered. Employees can also be a constant flow of ideas, drawing from previous experience and education.

Employees who feel they've been included in a plan or program are more likely to cooperate fully. Giving a goal for improving the operations and making the business more environmentally friendly can ignite untold ideas for long-term success. Employees are also more likely to accept and embrace changes when they've been given a role and responsibility to the process. This often means breaking down barriers between departments and bringing everyone into the fold.

Sometimes all it takes is acknowledging the cost and environmental impact for employees to look at operations just a little differently. Think about rewarding employees who offer suggestions on ways to save or implement programs in their departments. Make good examples of those advocating greener operations. Engaging your employees works.

CREATE A CLIMATE-FRIENDLY ZONE

Most think of going green at the office in terms of supplies, like recycled paper or changing out printer cartridges in a manner for safe disposal. But creative technologies can take your efforts even further, saving you and your staff time and money as well. Uptown Studios, a graphic design firm in Sacramento, California, is helping clients reduce their paper load by replacing their frequently used forms with electronic, downloadable online forms. Imagine if your new physician e-mailed you all the new patient forms that most require, allowing you to complete them online. Not only would it spare you the twenty minutes to fill out the forms when you arrive for your appointment—it would also save on time and costs for the physician to produce those forms. The bonus for the environment is less waste and less destruction of our forests, as well as all the harmful processing that is created in the manufacturing. Every day, creative people in the business environment are stretching their minds to produce better, more efficient, and planet-friendly ways of getting the job done. And who knows—perhaps, like Uptown Studios, you can open up a whole new revenue stream in the process.

When it comes to making purchases for the company, buy sustainable. Almost any office supply is available in recycled or organic versions, from sticky notes to calendars. Large office-supply retailers carry a variety of recycled-content paper products including folders and pencils. Other more specialized stores raise the bar for environmentally friendly supplies and equipment. They carry everything from hole punches made from recycled steel to hemp planners.

Make sure that the paper purchased is made from either 100 percent recycled fibers or at least a percentage of recycled fibers. Make sure that all of the office equipment is energy efficient with the Energy Star emblem. Take a little time when the next orders are placed to check out the environmental alternatives.

Allow equipment to be shared, such as printers, when it's realistic and won't hinder performance. Consider all the different processes that make up the day-to-day operations of the company and you will realize that little steps add up. When sending out mailings that need to be returned, use reusable envelopes. If possible, reuse envelopes you receive. If giving out promotional gifts, make sure they are made of recycled material. Review everyday practices for mailings and cut out any waste in the process. Can packages going to different people at the same address be combined? Can packages from different departments be shipped together? It may take some additional communication, but with support that travels all the way up the corporate ladder, savings can be seen in this area.

DISCIPLINED ACTION

There are so many options and venues for recycling at the office that it's a good idea to appoint one person as the recycling coordinator. This could be the same person who conducted the waste assessment or audit, but depending on the size of the business, this doesn't necessarily need to be his or her only responsibility. This coordinator should be someone who is enthusiastic about recycling and who is either already familiar with the company's waste management practices or is willing to jump right in—so to speak. Explain that the coordinator will be responsible for preparing a plan, educating coworkers, and determining a method for evaluating performance.

It's better to start off recycling only a few items and then adding to the list. Other aspects to consider when preparing a recycling plan are the haulers in your area. Some may come by to collect materials while others may require that you deliver the items to them. Also, the recycling coordinator will need to decide if it's best to separate the recyclables or comingle them; both methods have pros and cons.

Consider joining other offices in the area and expanding your recycling efforts. Also, see about participating in a cooperative that could not only get better prices in purchasing recycling equipment—but could also make the difference between paying to have your recyclables picked up and making money from them.

Smaller haulers may also be available at better rates than larger haulers for taking away materials. Secondhand hauling is also a great source. When office supplies or another item is delivered to the office, the hauler may be able to take the recyclables to a recycling facility for you.

Some common office items that can be recycled include:

- Aluminum cans
- Batteries (if rechargeable batteries aren't used)
- Cardboard boxes
- Computers
- Ink cartridges
- Magazines
- Paper
- Plastics and glass

REDUCE PACKAGING, REDUCE ATTACHMENT

With a successful recycling program underway, revisit your packaging and waste practices. You may be able to decrease the size of your dumpster or the frequency of disposal because of the reduction in the amount of material thrown away.

This may mean actually dumping out a trash bin and looking at the contents. See what's being thrown away and consider what kind of reductions can be made. This will give you a good idea of how much money and resources are lost every day.

Itemize the different components of the waste stream and determine what can realistically be reduced. Appoint one person to conduct the survey and evaluate the options.

Here are some common ways to reduce waste in the office:

- Go paperless. Encourage employees to use electronic means to work and communicate. You will inevitably have to use some paper, so start a recycling program. If your company does not generate enough recycling for your municipality to pick it up, set out boxes yourself and take them home for recycling. Make double-sided copies for handouts at meetings to conserve the amount of paper you use. An added bonus of a paperless office is less clutter, which allows for purposeful energy to expand and relieve stress.

- Choose your printer inks and toners carefully. Reuse and refill toners; recycle ink cartridges.
- Reuse office equipment. If you choose to upgrade your computer system, you'll be left with fully functioning machines that still have a lot of life in them. Donate them to charities or give them back to your supplier instead of throwing them away.
- Cut down on disposable products. If your business has a kitchen, a cafeteria, or a coffee machine, encourage employees to bring their own mugs and silverware.
- Reuse boxes and other shipping and packaging materials.
- Reuse old envelopes for interoffice mail.

These simple suggestions can be accomplished relatively painlessly. Tailor them to your company's needs to make them more effective.

THE ENERGY FACTOR

A first step in the direction of reducing the company's impact on the environment is to have an energy audit done for the facility. By cutting back the electricity demands from the business, you can reduce the need to burn coal or other nonrenewable power sources. You'll also be cutting back on the pollution generated as part of the power to electricity process.

The local power company may offer to perform an audit for a modest fee or possibly for free, but you may have to contract with an energy expert. You may spend some money in the beginning, but you'll save money in the end.

When hiring a contractor to perform an energy audit, make sure you know what you are signing up for. A preliminary audit includes just a walk-through with recommendations. A general audit goes further and includes a review of expenses. An investment audit will calculate the return on investment that can be expected, allowing businesses to budget building and operation renovations.

Before bringing in someone else, you can do your own energy walk-through, taking note of the following things:

- Is natural lighting used as much as possible?
- What kind of lighting is used?
- Can lights be replaced with compact fluorescent lamps or halogen lamps?
- Can green power be purchased from the local utility?
- Is the office equipment (e.g., computers, printers, fax machines) Energy Star rated?
- Are computers set to go to sleep?
- Are employees encouraged to turn off their computers, printers, and lights at the end of the day or if they will be gone for a few hours?
- Are outdoor windows and doors kept closed? Have windows been treated for energy efficiency?
- Is a comfortable temperature maintained for most employees?

It's understood that some employees may occasionally need to don a sweater to warm up and use a fan to cool off. A professional energy auditor will have more recommendations than one from a utility and will mostly include construction or material suggestions. After the audit, you will have to decide which improvements can be made, when they can be made, or when they can be scheduled into the capital-improvement budget.

THE NOBLE TRUTHS OF PAPER AND INK

Since the onset of personal computers, the amount of paper generated has skyrocketed. Not only is paper a waste product; it's expensive to buy and diminishes natural resources. By reducing the amount of paper used in the office, you can reduce the amount of paper needed to be stored and delivered. Come up with milestone goals for the percentage reduction in paper used.

Encourage employees to think first before printing and make sure all documents are spell-checked and formatted correctly. When making copies, double-side the documents. If you are producing handouts for a meeting, consider whether they are really necessary. When audiovisuals are used, paper handouts are usually superfluous. If handouts are a must, consider printing double pages on a single side of paper.

On average, every American uses 700 pounds of paper each year; that amount has doubled since 1960. The environmental impacts from using so much paper start with getting the fiber to the mill, manufacturing the paper from the fiber, and handling the paper after it's been used.

Encourage employees to use electronic mail rather than printing memos. Maintain electronic copies of company directories, manuals, and other material rather than printing hard copies for each person to shelve. Determine what activities can be accomplished through online programs rather than generating a paper trail. Office supplies can be ordered, conference or training requests submitted, and even timesheets and expense reports completed online. Not only does this save time, eliminating the need to shuttle paper from one desk to another—it saves resources too.

Other ways to cut back while maintaining a professional appearance include minimizing margins, decreasing font size, and eliminating double-spacing. These minor changes will add up over time, especially when printing large documents.

When looking at how your company can reduce paper, check in the recycle bins and trash cans. Is paper being thrown away that could be placed in the recycling bins? Is paper being tossed in the recycling bins that could be used for printing draft documents or for scrap paper? Are blank pages inserted as holding places in documents and then tossed into the bin with other scrap paper?

Give paper a second life. Beyond recycling, consider what else can be done with scrap paper. Can employees use it for notes, or can local schools use it in their classrooms? Can employees take it home to use in their computers and printers or for their children to use for coloring? Additionally, paper left over from shredders can be used as packing materials for shipping fragile items.

Printers may be inexpensive, but cartridges are not. Ink can be a costly part of any office operation. There are a number of ways to reduce its use. When printing a document that is not final, print it in draft mode. There is also software available that allows more control over the amount of ink a printer uses. The draft mode on your printer uses approximately 50 percent of the ink used in normal print mode, so although using the software may not save as much ink as printing in draft mode, it does offer some in-between options.

A CLEANER JOURNEY

Even with the advent of online meetings and teleconferencing, people are still flying and driving an extensive amount. If a trip out of the office is necessary, consider more fuel-efficient ways of traveling or combining trips to handle more than one meeting. Sometimes, juggling a schedule can reduce travel from two trips to one.

Carpooling

Employers can provide special parking spots for those who carpool. This is particularly valuable if the office is large or parking is scarce. Carpooling must be defined to employees and may include stipulations that at least two people must share the commute for at least half the distance.

Public Transportation

When it comes to getting employees to and from work, encourage the use of mass transit where available. Employers can provide tax-advantage spending accounts for employees to cover the cost of riding the bus or taking the train or subway. These programs allow employees to pay for mass transit with pretax dollars using a convenient pass or card that's ordered online. Companies like Wage-Works, Inc. institute programs like these. WageWorks also maintains a database of transportation services available across the country.

Hybrids

Choose energy-efficient vehicles or hybrids as your company cars or fleet vehicles. Companies will feel the savings on multiple cars more than individuals. Not only will this save money; it will also set an example of conservation and environmental protection at a corporate level.

Telecommuting

Telecommuting has also become popular and saves on more than transportation costs. Some companies are strictly set up for telecommuting, using field representatives or contractors who work out of their residences. When compared to going in to the office, there are other benefits in working from home. Depending on the company dress code, allowing employees to work from home can decrease the cost and environmental impact from dry cleaning.

CHAPTER FOURTEEN

Green Entertaining

Central to a life of Zen is gratitude. In this age of commercialization, many families are scaling back on holiday gatherings. But green entertaining is an opportunity to expand your gratitude, loving-kindness, and holiday cheer through simple, cost-effective decorating and gift giving. All it takes is a little Zen contemplation, planning, and joyous creativity. It's the perfect opportunity to get everyone in your family involved for some good enlightened fun.

No matter what the holiday, it's likely to come with pressures to shop, decorate, give gifts, and feed friends and family. It helps to take a step back early on and think about what the occasion really means—and how you can celebrate without doing too much damage to the planet.

SIMPLE, SPIRITUAL HOLIDAYS

The stretch on the calendar between Thanksgiving and New Year's Day includes a variety of different celebrations. It's a time of year that marks the viability of the economy. Forecasts for holiday shopping start in the fall, and critiques of how much shoppers spent ring in the New Year.

The holidays bring families and friends together, but there is a lot of stress over excess spending, hectic schedules, and the potential to overindulge. The holidays also generate a lot of waste. If you want to scale back, you don't need to change years of tradition, but a little cutting equals less environmental impact.

When looking at ways to simplify, consider starting with decorations. If your family purchases a Christmas tree, a living tree might be a good choice. Living trees can be purchased and planted after the holidays are over. Buying an artificial tree means it can be used over and over again. If you don't have a place to plant a living tree but want the authenticity of a real tree, make sure to recycle your cut tree.

When you put up ornaments, let the tree show. If some needles show after all the ornaments are hung, that's okay. Not every branch needs to be glittering and sparkly. If you need more ornaments, consider making them from recycled materials. There are tons of websites and library books with great ideas for ornaments, and if you remember to date your new ornaments you can look back and reminisce every year.

When lighting up inside or out, lower-wattage lights can bring about the same glitter and gleam without the expense. Not only do smaller lights burn less electricity; they also produce less heat, making them safer. Light-emitting diode (LED) holiday lights are new on the scene. They cost about $8 more than a standard strand but will last up to ten years and use less electricity. Remember to put your lights on a timer so they automatically shut off.

When it comes to partying, consider swapping cookies instead of gifts. If you plan a cookie exchange, have guests share stories about their recipes. Was it a hand-me-down from a beloved aunt or a brand-new recipe from an easy cooking guide? Some hosts ask guests to bring a dozen cookies for each guest, but you can adjust the numbers as you like. Your flexibility and creativity as a host will foster a festive atmosphere for everyone.

Once the last present is unwrapped and the last guest leaves, it's time to clean up. Make sure to keep the reusable items like decorations and table settings. Pack them with newspaper and shredded junk mail. Keep any cards that can be used next year.

HOLISTIC HALLOWEEN

It's a scary time of year filled with costumes and candy. The costume market has exploded as children and grownups dress like their favorite movie and TV characters. But, before splurging on a costume that may only be worn once, consider what's in the closet. See if there is anything that can be modified and mixed up to be used as a costume. Leftover 1980s clothes or an old sport coat can be the beginning of a retro-theme costume. Overalls and a plaid shirt can be the basis for a farm or scarecrow costume. All it takes is an old dress or uniform and some scissors and makeup. If your closets aren't serving up any costume ideas, visit a local consignment or thrift shop.

When the trick-or-treating is over, save the costumes and consider having a swap at a local elementary school next year. Not only will you be recycling the costumes—this may be a great way to provide costumes for families who can't afford to purchase them. Old costumes can also be kept in dress-up bins and trunks. Grownups can mix and match or even swap costumes down the road.

Scary jack-o'-lanterns yield a lot of waste. Don't throw your pumpkin's guts away after you're done carving. Use the meat to make muffins or a pie, then salt and bake the seeds for a delicious snack. When the jack-o'-lantern has seen his last day, toss him on the compost pile instead of throwing him to the curb.

This may sound cheap, but don't go overboard giving out candy. It's rare for kids to go home without candy spilling out of their buckets and bags. More candy given out means more candy bought, and the more candy bought means the more candy made and the more waste produced. Depending on how much trick-or-treating traffic you have, you may be stuck with leftovers. Consider donating candy to a shelter or keeping it for another holiday down the road. If well-sealed or frozen, candy can keep for months.

A Conscious Greeting

It's more of a tradition with winter holidays, but that doesn't stop stationers from promoting more and more special occasion cards. Forgo the Halloween and St. Patrick's Day cards altogether if you're seeking to be greener, or consider sending e-cards to friends and family.

Holiday cards don't have to be thrown away as soon as the occasion passes. They can be made into a variety of useful items. Fronts can be reused to make new cards, bookmarks, gift tags, and lace-up toys.

If sending cards or holiday letters just isn't a tradition you are willing to give up, consider sending only a letter. Use hand stamps to make it festive. Another alternative is to purchase cards from your favorite charity. Choose an organization that sends a message you support and that uses recycled materials.

Giving Responsibly

Gifts are integral to most holidays and special occasions, but take a minute to think before you purchase. Don't buy a token gift that will soon be forgotten just because you feel obligated. Think about what resources it took to make and package the gift and what will become of it after the special day. It's not that you should feel guilty when making a purchase, but it is worth considering where it came from, where it will go, and how it fits into the whole scheme of things.

Purchasing Purposefully

Gifts made with love can be particularly sweet. Knowing someone made homemade soap or jewelry really adds a personal touch to the holiday or occasion. When shopping, eliminate or reduce the number of plastic bags you bring home. Take along your own bags or double up your purchases by putting them in bags you already have from other stores.

Consider gifts of entertainment or endowment. Tickets to a stage show, sporting event, or a movie don't require excess packaging or wrapping. An evening out might be the perfect gift. Donations to a favorite charity are something to think about too. A commemorative brick or the care and feeding of a seabird may be a very special gift for someone who has everything.

When buying a gift, shop green. Look for items that encourage conservation and sustainable living. There are plenty of websites promoting sustainable products. Consider buying friends and family canvas bags to take shopping or items made from recycled materials like street signs or old album covers. Chances are there won't be any awkward duplicates with unique recycled gifts. Do a good deed. Instead of buying a gift for neighbors or relatives, do something nice. Rake their lawn, shovel their sidewalk, or take on another chore. This is particularly nice if they really don't want anything. Some people would rather not be given gifts that they must find a place for or figure out what to do with. This is the perfect opportunity to make frozen meals, put together an emergency kit, give a gift certificate for a nearby grocery store, or make a gift basket of essentials like stamps, envelopes, and pens. Don't forget about photos—put them in a small book or on a magnet or mug.

Look around you. Is there something you have that you know someone would enjoy receiving? Give a decorative bowl from your own hutch or a book from your bookshelf to make a nice gift. This makes for a great opportunity to regift too. If you can't return a gift, leave it boxed up and go shopping in your closet the next time you need a gift (no wallet required).

Wrapping Wisely

You've picked out the perfect gift. Now what? Consider a reusable bag or box to wrap the present. For paper options, try comics, maps, coloring pages, or wrapping made from recycled paper. Use scarves to secure a gift. The wrapping can even be part of the gift, using containers like flower pots and dishes. For gift tags, cut up used greeting or holiday cards so the art on the card serves as the front of the gift tag and write a message on the back. If there is writing on the back, just glue a piece of paper with your message over it.

Wrapping presents has been a custom since the Chinese invented papermaking in 105 C.E. In the United States, tissue paper was routinely used to wrap presents. In 1917, the Hall brothers ran out of the traditional tissue paper and sold decorative envelope liners for wrapping presents instead. The idea obviously caught on.

When sending gifts, try to reuse shipping materials like padded envelopes, cartons, and peanuts, and think about how the gift will be sent when you're shopping for it. Smaller and lighter may be easier and greener to package and send. If the gift is staying local, avoid wrapping altogether. Hide the gift and send the recipient on a scavenger hunt to retrieve it.

Planning a Green Gathering

Entertaining can vary from an extended visit from out-of-town friends and family to a fancy one-night shindig. If the evening requires entertaining a large group of people, turn the heat down before your guests arrive. Having lots of people in the house creates a lot of body heat.

Depending on the theme, consider whether decorating is necessary. If you do need some zing, make your decorations. Create banners from recycled newsprint. Homemade banners are much more personal than mass-produced ones, and large rolls of recycled newsprint can be used for the banner and then reused as drawing paper throughout the year. One way to make birthday party decorations more special is to make a photo collage of the birthday celebrant.

Conservative Cooking

Consider cutting behind-the-scenes corners that will conserve energy, natural resources, and money. For starters, don't overcook. Meals should be planned according to the guest list. Consider who will eat what and what portions are appropriate. Don't feel obligated to offer guests every potential appetizer or entrée under the sun, and there's no need to overfeed guests either. The holiday season is a time most people struggle with temptation and add extra pounds, so eliminating enticements may not be such a bad idea.

Don't throw leftovers away. Send them home with guests, pack them into your own refrigerator or freezer, or donate them to a shelter. Turkey carcasses and ham bones make for great soup. If there is a whole pie or untouched leftover, donate it to a local food bank.

If leftovers outlive their useful life in the fridge, add them to the compost bin. However, meat and processed foods are not good for a compost bin because they can attract rodents.

The Dharma of Dishes

It may mean extra work for you, but think about hosting the event with reusable dishes instead of disposable dishes. If it's a particularly formal event, borrow or rent dishes rather than buying them. When washing up after the affair, fully load the dishwasher to get the most out of the hot water. Put out separate bins for recyclables and label them so guests know where to toss their glass, plastic, and aluminum.

CHAPTER FIFTEEN

Transportation with Purpose

Zen is about finding where your comfort zones are, challenging them, and trying something new...expanding your mind and physical limitations for a more purposeful end. Your daily commute may not seem as if it could lead you to Nirvana, but taking right action by stepping out of your comfort zone and switching your mode of transportation to a more environmentally friendly option could lead you to open your mind to a new truth.

Daily commutes, errands, weekend trips—everyone has somewhere to go. Different methods of travel have varying degrees of impact on the environment. This chapter delves into the different energy-efficient and eco-friendly transportation alternatives that are becoming increasingly available and more popular. Tips are offered on alternative ways to get around and to green the rides you already own.

THE WISDOM OF YOUR VEHICLE CHOICE

If you're considering getting a new car, think about what the Buddha would buy! Here are some alternatives to the common gas guzzler.

Hybrids

A hybrid by definition is a combination of two separate things—in the case of automobiles, an engine and a motor. A hybrid car uses both an electric motor and a gasoline engine. Both the engine and motor have favorable and less savory qualities, but when working together they bring out the best in each other. Electric cars are becoming more common and produce fewer to no emissions—a great benefit. Gasoline-powered cars have the pickup most drivers are accustomed to and they can be conveniently fueled, but gasoline isn't the cleanest fuel. Producing it isn't good for the environment and neither is burning it.

Gasoline combustion engines produce a host of contaminants such as volatile organic compounds, nitrogen oxides, carbon monoxide, and carbon dioxide. The United States consumes approximately 25 percent of all the oil used in any given day—20.8 million gallons. The US Energy Information Administration (EIA) estimates that in 2015 American drivers burned about 140.4 billion gallons of gasoline. The EIA forecasts increases of about 1 percent a year for the foreseeable future.

In hybrid vehicles, the electric and gasoline systems work together, using each other's best aspects. The gas engine can charge the batteries. Hybrids capture the energy produced during braking, so they don't have to be plugged in to recharge their batteries. Because gasoline motors are so inefficient at low speeds, the electric motors kick in during stop-and-go traffic, significantly reducing the amount of fuel burned and emissions produced. For skeptics who are concerned that hybrid-car batteries are too expensive to replace and dispose of, rest assured. Ford, Honda, and Toyota claim that the batteries in their hybrids will last the life of the vehicle. When it comes to disposal, the batteries can be recycled just like any other car battery.

The EPA is arming consumers with more accurate information when it comes to fuel efficiency. It seems consumers weren't getting accurate mileage information, in part because driving patterns have changed since the testing protocols were developed in the early 1970s, so the EPA is devising better ways to determine accurate fuel efficiency that mimic realistic driving conditions. The new values have been required since the 2008 models.

Hybrids, when compared to their gasoline-powered counterparts, get about 20 to 35 percent better gas mileage, but the improved fuel efficiency may not make up for the increased sticker price. For example, look at a side-by-side comparison of the 2020 models of Honda's Civic Hybrid sedan and its traditional Civic sedan.

According to Honda, its Civic Hybrid gets 48 miles to the gallon in city driving and 51 miles to the gallon on the highway, averaging out to 47 miles to the gallon. The base price is $29,600. The 2020 Civic Hybrid may be eligible for a federal tax credit of as much as $2,100, and individual states may offer additional tax incentives. The hybrid's sibling, the gas-powered Civic sedan, gets an average of 31 miles to the gallon and has a base price of $24,000. Taking the maximum federal tax credit for the hybrid into account, the difference in price between the two cars is $5,490. The hybrid will need to refuel less often, which will save its owner money, but the amount of time it will take to close the $5,490 price gap depends on the cost of gas and how often the tank needs to be refilled. A rough estimate: If the price of gas averages $2.50 per gallon (adjusted for inflation), and the cars are each driven 15,000 miles per year, the hybrid will take a little more than thirteen years to earn its higher price tag back. The website www.fueleconomy.gov, run by the US Department of Energy and the EPA, allows browsers to do their own comparisons and view emissions statistics. The price of a hybrid might be higher, but it also includes the cost of developing new technology.

The fuel efficiency and price of the car aren't the only things to consider when buying a greener car. Hybrids produce much fewer emissions than cars that run strictly on gasoline. According to the fuel economy website, the Honda Civic will produce about 5.5 tons per year of greenhouse gases, or carbon dioxide equivalents, while the Honda Civic Hybrid will produce 3.7 tons per year.

A side-by-side comparison can't be made on the first mass-produced and dominant hybrid on the market, the Toyota Prius, because there is no gas-powered version. By 2016 Prius had sold almost two million vehicles, roughly 48 percent of hybrid sales in the US. However, by 2019 sales have been falling in the face of brisk competition.

Flex-Fuel Vehicles

Flexible-fuel vehicles, or FFVs, are made to run on a mixture of gasoline and an alternate fuel such as ethanol or methanol. Standard gasoline engines can't operate using flex fuels, but FFVs can burn both—and that's what makes them so flexible. There are a variety of FFVs on the market, including sedans, trucks, and sport utility vehicles.

Ethanol—otherwise known as ethyl alcohol, grain alcohol, or moonshine—leads the way in replacing a portion of the gasoline. It's made by distilling a fermented brew of corn, yeast, sugar, and water. Other plants, such as switchgrass, are being considered as corn substitutes. It takes one bushel of corn to produce $2\frac{1}{2}$ gallons of ethanol. There is concern that the environmental impact from growing plants to produce ethanol (i.e., from the use of fertilizers and pesticides, and the transportation of plants to processing facilities) outweighs the benefits of burning cleaner fuels. The most common mixtures using ethanol are E10 and E85, where the number accounts for the percentage of ethanol in the mixture compared to gasoline. Gasoline is still needed because ethanol isn't volatile enough to ignite. E10, comprised of 10 percent ethanol, is used more for an octane enhancer, while E85 is considered a full-fledged alternative fuel. Ethanol burns cleaner, significantly reducing emissions.

Stations selling E85 are in short supply. Make sure when purchasing an FFV that you consider where you will be traveling and how that compares to where E85 stations are located. Also consider how your car will run on gasoline if you are ever in a situation where there is no alternative. Alternative fueling locations can be found at www.afdc.energy.gov.

There are a variety of ethanol-fueled cars available; Ford and General Motors are the major manufacturers. Ford offers the Crown Victoria, Mercury Grand Marquis, Lincoln Town Car, and F-150 pickup truck in E85 options. GM offers Suburbans and Yukons, along with a Chevy Police Tahoe. Because fueling stations are limited, FFVs can be better suited for public and private fleets where E85 can be supplied at a set location.

A less-popular fuel alternative is methanol or wood alcohol, which is made primarily from natural gas or methane. M85, the most common methanol additive, must be stored either as a compressed gas or a liquid. Significant amounts of electricity are needed to compress and liquefy the gas. Methanol had its day back in the late 1980s and 1990s when California led the charge in using this alternative fuel, although it was never really embraced by the rest of the United States.

Alternative Fuel Vehicles

Where FFVs rely on ethanol and methanol as a fuel component, alternative fuel vehicles (AFVs) rely on a combination of gasoline and either compressed natural gas (CNG) or liquefied petroleum gas (LPG). As with other alternatives, fueling station locations are spotty across the United States. Most AFVs on the road were converted from standard gasoline-powered engines. Tax incentives encourage companies to convert their fleets and private individuals to convert their personal cars. Some states even allow drivers of certified AFVs to use high-occupancy lanes.

Scooters

Scooter sales are skyrocketing as people look for a break from high gas prices. Scooter prices range anywhere from $1,000 to $10,000; fuel ratings for gas-powered scooters run 50 miles to the gallon or better. There's a true distinction in size and power; smaller scooters are slower and not as powerful. New larger scooters compare to motorcycles in price and power while still offering a low mileage alternative. Unlike motorcycles, scooters allow drivers to sit upright without throwing a leg over and straddling the seat.

Electric scooters range from the foldup push scooter to a full sit-down model. Unlike gas-powered scooters, electrics are allowed on mass transit, making a commute to the bus stop a little quicker. At a sticker price of $500 or less, they're much cheaper. Electric scooters require four to eight hours of charging and will take drivers about 5 miles. They travel at approximately 10 miles per hour and can be weak on hills. Depending on what riders need, scooters can be an excellent way to get across campus or to the train depot. When it comes to the environment, no exhaust means no air pollution. With proper maintenance and operation, battery life spans increase. Smaller scooters fall under moped regulations, while the bigger scooters are legally considered motorcycles and require a special license endorsement. Drivers should always take care because although driving a scooter is fun, crashing is not. Proper shoes and a helmet should always be worn.

Hybrid scooters are new on the scene and operate using electric batteries and gasoline. Use of a battery reduces gas consumption, and the battery can charge while it's under gas power. The combination allows drivers to switch to electric and access buildings or covered areas where gasoline-powered scooters aren't allowed. Because they have gas tanks and are larger than electric scooters, transporting them on mass transit isn't an option.

AN ALTERNATIVE PATH

When fueling your car or deciding how to get to work in the morning, consider what the Buddha would do to travel without harming the environment.

Biodiesel

Diesel fuel is produced as part of the process of refining regular gasoline. Diesel fuel gets better gas mileage than standard gasoline and produces less carbon dioxide. Unfortunately, diesel releases a lot of particulate matter that gets stuck in people's noses and lungs, even impacting the body's ability to transfer oxygen to the blood. The EPA estimates that ninety million people currently live in areas with elevated levels of diesel fuel particulate matter. While petroleum diesel is a fuel-efficient alternative to standard gasoline, it's still not very Earth friendly.

That's where biodiesel comes in. Made from renewable resources like vegetable oil, animal fats, even used cooking oil, biodiesel uses alcohol to separate nonfuel components from fat. Production ranges from full-scale facilities to home kits that can be built and operated in the backyard. By-products of the process include glycerol—the same ingredient that's used in making soap, toothpaste, food, and cosmetics—and seed meal that can be used in livestock feed. The exhaust from biodiesel smells good. If the fuel is made from corn or feedstock, the exhaust can smell like popcorn or doughnuts.

Biodiesel can be mixed from ratios of B5 to B100. The numbers stand for how much of the mixture is biodiesel. For example, the B5 mixture is 5 percent biodiesel and 95 percent petroleum-based diesel. Significant benefits can be seen when using as low a mixture as B20. Substituting biodiesel doesn't reduce engine power, but it does burn cleaner, reducing both carbon monoxide and carbon dioxide emissions. Biodiesel does produce more nitrous oxide than traditional fuels, but the emissions can be controlled or offset using catalytic converters.

Being Your Own Motor

While cars may be the most popular mode of transportation, there are other alternatives. With environmental and health concerns as primary factors, more and more people are biking and walking to get around. Drivers take 1.1 billion trips every day. Based on information collected by the Bureau of Transportation Statistics, the majority of those trips, about 87 percent, are taken in personal vehicles. If each driver cut out one trip a day—or even a few a week—it would save up to 25 percent of the fossil fuels used for personal transportation.

An Awakening Is Afoot

Older generations lament their daily treks to school, walking uphill both ways in the snow. Today, fewer children walk to and from school, and when they do it's rarely uphill both ways. Walking usually takes more time than driving. As trip distances increased and busy schedules became the norm, most people turned to personal automobiles. Still, if you are looking to do the planet (and your body) a favor, you can walk to the grocery store for milk or to a friend's house for a visit.

When opting to walk instead of drive, there are a few things you can do to make it more comfortable. Quick-drying clothing means no more sweaty shirts, and carrying a water bottle will keep you hydrated. Lightweight daypacks are great for toting items that will be taken along or picked up on errands. Consider safety when you choose to walk. Choose a route that's well lit and pedestrian-friendly, and take a cell phone. Even though you aren't driving, it's a good idea to take a driver's license or other form of identification.

Bicycling Bliss

Biking is good exercise—one trip on the bike saves one trip in a car. Many cities are not set up for safe biking, but improvements are being made. The city of Davis, California, boasts more bicycles than cars with wide streets and a network of bike paths. Davis's mild climate and gentle terrain encourages bike travel, which the city estimates makes up 20 to 25 percent of all trips. In 2010 Davis became home to the US Bicycling Hall of Fame.

Bikers need to know the laws in their area and be careful when sharing the road with cars. In many states, bicyclists can a receive a ticket and points on their driver's license when breaking the law, such as failing to yield at a stop sign or peddling the wrong way down a one-way street. Another safety note: Bicycling under the influence is never a good idea.

Respecting the Car Pool Lane

Not everybody has to have a car. There are a lot of opportunities to share rides with one other person or with a whole bunch. If you live in an area where riding mass transit isn't feasible but still want to take a car or two off the road, consider carpooling. A number of websites and apps match destinations and people looking to save money and vehicle use. Check out sites like www.icarpool.com and www.rideshareonline.com, and apps like eRideShare.

Not only does ridesharing offer companionship and a break from always having to be behind the wheel; many states also have carpool lanes. These high-occupancy vehicle lanes allow cars to sidestep traffic for a less congested ride.

Depending on how long the commute is, riders may be spending a lot of time together, so it's best to set a few rules at the get-go:

- Where will drivers and riders meet? Will it be at someone's house or a common location like a parking lot?
- Is smoking acceptable? Some people may not mind being around smoke if it's in someone else's car while others may choose not to expose themselves to smoke at all.
- Is eating in the car okay?
- Are stops acceptable?
- Will there be a set wait time if someone is late?

Some websites allow rideshares to select criteria, filtering out certain elements. If everyone in the carpool drives equal miles, then the costs will be even, but if one person is the sole driver, the costs will need to be split. The American Automobile Association (AAA) calculated in 2013 that every mile a person drives costs $0.60.8. This accounts for gas, insurance, and maintenance. So when one person drives more or is the only driver, it's fair to ask others sharing the ride to pony up.

Sharing Cars

Car sharing has increased as well, and there are a variety of programs available. Businesses like Zipcar (www.zipcar.com) operate in numerous cities across the United States, including New York, Chicago, and Los Angeles. Cooperatives like Getaround (www.getaround.com) in San Francisco operate as nonprofits. With car-sharing programs, members pay a monthly fee or hourly rates and have access to a variety of cars and trucks. You choose whatever vehicle suits your fancy, a truck for that trip to the lumberyard or a sedan for a night out with friends. Most programs offer a fleet of hybrid and low-emission vehicles too.

Estimates for the number of personal vehicles taken off the road for each shared vehicle ranges from four to ten depending on how many people share the car. Car sharing encourages people to drive more efficiently because they're either limited to hours offered by their plan or paying for each hour. Costs of the program include gas and insurance (and sometimes perks like satellite radio), and members don't have to bother with parking their own car or taking it in for repair work.

On the Journey Together

Mass transit helps reduce the number of cars on the road. Numbers vary, but the Maryland Department of Transportation estimates that a full bus eliminates sixty cars on the road and that translates to reduced emissions to the air and runoff to streams and creeks. You can find out more about the bus service in your area by contacting the local transit authority or by looking online for schedules and routes.

Taking the bus allows riders time to read, listen to music, or even catch up on sleep on the way to work or school. Bus rides can also be substitutes for long car trips. Greyhound and Trailways buses travel across the country, allowing riders to check out vistas along the way. Before making a trip, ask about meal stops and consider bringing along a pillow and snacks to make the trip more enjoyable.

According to the American Public Transportation Association, public transportation replaces personal cars and trips and reduces emissions. For every mile a passenger rides on public transportation rather than driving a car, 95 percent less carbon monoxide, 90 percent fewer volatile organic compounds, and 50 percent less carbon dioxide and nitrogen oxides are produced.

A Spacious Mind for Reducing Emissions

For those times when you do drive, you can take steps to increase your car's gas mileage and even reduce emissions. Remember—the more gas a car uses, the more harmful its emissions are.

The Environmental Protection Agency calculated that the average mileage only increased .2 miles per gallon (mpg) in 2017, to 24.9 mpg. The improvement could have been greater, but the huge popularity of SUVs, relatively inexpensive gas, and more people idling in traffic brought down the mileage calculations (but did not decrease emissions).

Until zero-impact cars or fuels are invented, here's a list of things you can do to improve fuel efficiency:

- Aggressive driving, including rapid acceleration off the line and through traffic, wastes gas and increases emissions. Maintaining a smooth—and legal—pace will get you more miles to the gallon.
- Every car reaches its optimal fuel efficiency at a different speed, but it's generally around 60 miles per hour. According to the US Department of Energy, for every 5 miles an hour you drive over 60 mph, it's like you are spending an extra 20 cents per gallon of gas.

- Carrying heavy loads reduces a car's gas mileage. It makes more of a difference in smaller cars than larger ones because the weight carried is relative to the weight of the car.
- Idling, burning gas, and getting nowhere. If you need another reason to avoid drive-through windows, consider this. Idling for longer than a minute or two actually uses more gas than starting the car, except in the case of hybrids. If you just have to get that burger and fries, you can park and walk inside instead.

Properly maintained engines operate more efficiently and get better gas mileage. Air filters remove impurities from the air before they can reach the car's engine. Clogged filters can allow some impurities to get through and reduce gas mileage. Finally, properly inflated tires are not only safer to drive on—they improve mileage too.

CHAPTER SIXTEEN

The Zen Traveler Leaves No Trace

Zen is a tradition of compassion, outreach, and good humor. The Zen traveler is an explorer, both near and far, seeking unique treasures of the soul and spirit, and the mind and body. By combining tradition with contemporary opportunities, today's Zen traveler is presented with endless possibilities to both learn and teach, expand their horizons while conserving resources and, ultimately, enjoy the journey to its fullest.

There's no better way to appreciate the planet and all it has to offer than by going out and experiencing it firsthand. Increasing numbers of opportunities allow vacationers to help the environment while having fun. This chapter explores the different travel options, from visiting exotic lands and locales to checking out what's right around the corner or in the backyard.

ADHERE TO A CONSCIOUS PATH

What makes a trip ecological, environmental, or green? Ecotourism meets three goals. It helps sustain the environment, the economy, and the culture of the area visited. Unless those three criteria are met, it may not be considered ecotourism.

Don't be taken in by the Green Globe logo. This circular award is given, or sold, by the American Society of Travel Agents to those travel destinations that agree to work toward more environmentally sound practices. Note that they agree to work toward sound practices; they don't have to achieve them. It's marketing at its most eco-friendly.

Tourism has become a global industry. Its popularity is such that even the United Nations has become involved with the Convention on Biological Diversity (CBD), which works to develop guidelines on biodiversity and sustainable tourism. Many locals who earn their living through tourism believe that global initiatives aren't necessary since the indigenous people have more at stake in maintaining their own environment. There is also concern that large organizations and corporations will develop areas for sustainable tourism while economically overpowering smaller local businesses.

Ecotourism comes in many shapes and sizes, from adventure trips for the highly skilled and proficiently athletic to the more relaxing, softer trips for those looking to experience nature without breaking a sweat.

Tourism Teachings

There are a variety of terms used in the eco-travel industry that may be confusing. Not all types of travel afford the same kind of environmental benefits to local people that true ecotourism does. Here's a rundown of the most common terms used:

- *Adventure tourism* is usually nature-oriented and involves some amount of risk, but not all trips require a specialized skill or the desire to rough it. Some tours are considered hard adventure, meaning participants are required to either paddle or hike in difficult conditions and for durations well beyond novice level. Soft tours allow travelers greater comfort and are not quite as challenging.
- *Geotourism* usually centers on the geographic nature of the environment. Tourism helps to enhance the environment along with culture and overall well-being of local residents. This could include a hiking tour of Auckland, New Zealand's urban volcanoes, or archaeology trips through the Shetland Islands.
- *Nature-based tourism* relies on the natural environment or settings to entice travelers. This could include jungle lodges as well as whale-watching cruise ships. These may or may not be environmentally friendly.

- *Sustainable tourism* protects the environment, meaning that travel will continue in the area without destruction of any habitat or damage to resources. The area's integrity will be maintained for future travelers. Is trophy hunting in southern Namibia a good example of sustainable tourism? No.

A Vibrant Relationship

When done right, ecotourism can help preserve or even remediate a locale. Not only does conscious tourism raise money; it also increases awareness of native cultures and the environment, bringing to life images from magazines or TV, adding touch, smell, and taste. It gives tourists a reason to protect an environment or a culture because they've experienced it firsthand.

Whether buying goods or purchasing services, the money spent usually goes at least in part to the local economy that supports indigenous cultures. When it comes to money, villages and communities rely on tourism so they don't have to turn to other sources of income like mining, drilling, and foresting that degrade their resources. Properly run lodges and low-impact tours can support an economy, proving an alternative for inhabitants to earn a living. Tourists can't visit the rain forests of Costa Rica if the trees have been cut down for lumber, and the leather craftsmen can't survive without tourists visiting the Otavalo Market of the Andes Highlands and purchasing their wares.

Seek Authenticity

Because of the increase in ecotourism, some unscrupulous guides, agents, or establishments will use the label for tourism that really doesn't meet the eco-criteria. This takes away from those promoting and relying on ecotourism. Not all adventure vacations, sustainable tours, or nature trips are 100 percent beneficial to the environment, and the term could be used as a marketing ploy to generate ticket sales. First, almost all travel involves the use of cars, planes, cruise ships, or other vehicles that depend on fossil fuels. Although tourists would be hard-pressed to avoid any degrading practices, minimizing them is possible. Also, while large crowds may spend a lot of money, they have negative impacts that must be considered. Crowds can inhibit certain animal behavior such as breeding, and trash generated from tourists can be costly if handled properly or dangerous to the environment if not.

Traveling Smart—Honoring the Path

When abiding by the true spirit of eco-travel, there are rules tourists can live by to make sure they are promoting the conservation of cultures, economics, and the environment. Treat locations as you would your home. While you may not live there, others do.

Study Up

To get the most out of travel, prepare for your trip before you ever leave home. Learn about your destination. If you are traveling to a non-English-speaking country, learn a handful of words in the local language. Respect is an important element of Zen and trying to communicate in someone else's native language relays a strong message.

Spend Locally

Whether for a tour guide, transportation, food, or souvenirs, purchases help the local community. By choosing local merchants, there is more opportunity to impact the economy and learn the culture. A local guide or scout can provide a wealth of knowledge, making the most of side trips. Take advantage of their knowledge by asking about other local places of interest. There's nothing like local advice to find the best restaurant and neighborhood hangout.

Take Nothing but Pictures

Everyone's heard it before. It is posted at park entrances and in guidebooks, but it bears repeating. "Take nothing but pictures; leave nothing but footprints." Awareness of your impact on the earth is important and everything you do has consequences. One small stone or shell may not seem like much, but repeated over and over again could leave a shore or stream barren. Leaving discards only means someone else will have to follow behind, picking up trash— or worse, it stays put to endanger an ecosystem.

Show Loving-Kindness

Don't be wasteful of a community's resources. Their water may be hard to come by, so use it sparingly. Other resources like wood and gasoline may be harder to get than you might think. Sustainable hotels or smaller inns may create less environmental impact than a larger commercial lodge.

Be Respectful

Tourists are visitors. Be respectful of the people who call your travel destinations home. Consider the clothes you wear and how you speak in public, even going one step further and learning about local culture, traditions, and customs.

THE JOURNEY: ONE OR MANY?

There are many ways to travel—alone or in groups, with friends, or with family. No matter what kind of trip you plan, do some research. Not only will you be able to make better use of your time and resources. It's always more enjoyable to be familiar with your surroundings—not to mention learning ahead makes for a great game of "Did you know?"

A Solo Meditation

You may be a planner ready to prepare your own eco-friendly vacation, possibly going with a group of friends or family or alone. Thanks to the Internet and local libraries, there are plenty of resources available to help plan a trip. Ask others who have visited the area what they liked most or what they would change if they traveled there again. See if they have any recommendations for must-do side trips. Also, consider contacting local guides or outfitters and ask questions. Using local businesses not only supports their economy; it often also gives you the best information. Many more people, especially women, are traveling alone these days. When traveling solo, take precautions. It's a good idea to leave an itinerary of where you are staying and to know ahead of time where you are headed. Solo travelers may want to hold off announcing to strangers that they are traveling alone.

The International Ecotourism Society (TIES) works with the Rainforest Alliance, helping both tourists and tour operators with sustainable travel. The organizations provide information to travelers on how to be a green tourist and on the different travel opportunities available. Check out bulletin boards online where travelers can share information on different trips they have made.

EDUCATED TRAVEL

Because eco-travel has become so popular, many travel agents include it in the gamut of trips they offer. Certain travel agents may specialize solely in eco-travel. Some may not understand the difference between eco-travel and adventure travel, leaving it up to the traveler to make the distinction. Contact these or other companies to find an eco-friendly travel agent:

- Preferred Adventures Ltd., www.preferredadventures.com
- Eco-Resorts, www.eco-resorts.com
- Adventure Life, www.adventure-life.com

GIVING BACK: HUMANITARIAN VACATIONS

If you are not one to kick back and relax, even during vacation, you may want to consider a working vacation. These vacations allow people to volunteer their time while experiencing another culture or environment. These trips could range from blazing trails and patrolling forests in national parks to recording whale migration patterns. They could be organized or sponsored by local churches, humanitarian groups, or volunteer networks that give those looking for the opportunity a chance to volunteer away from home.

The American Hiking Society organizes vacations where volunteers help rebuild paths, cabins, and shelters in parks in thirty different states. Vacation assignments cost members $100; nonmembers pay $130. Volunteers sleep at camp and hike to the work site every morning. Find more information at their website, www.americanhiking.org.

Even though travelers are working during their vacation, payment usually comes through the good karma of feeling rewarded. The cost of working or volunteer vacations is comparable to other vacations. Some websites offer tips on how to raise money to pay for humanitarian or working trips, and chances are that friends and family may be willing to contribute. Because of the volunteer nature of the trip and the work performed, the costs of working vacations are often tax-deductible.

A GROUP MEDITATION

If you aren't up to planning your own trip and would like to take advantage of having an expert on hand, consider booking a trip with an environmental group. Groups like the Sierra Club and The Nature Conservancy arrange trips all over the world. Trips usually include hiking, kayaking, horseback riding, and other activities and are led by an expert guide who shares information on the local environment and wildlife.

Like any other group activity, there may not be a lot of extra room in the schedule or flexibility for deviation or side trips, but travelers, especially those new to the locale, benefit by being led by a professional who knows the area and how to get around it. Combining all the travelers into one group eliminates the need for personal vehicles, which allows passengers to see the sites and get to know each other rather than navigating unknown territory.

PEACEFUL RETREATS

If you are looking for a Zen-like getaway, a relaxing retreat may fit the bill. Retreats are usually located in secluded areas. They can focus on themes such as wellness, yoga and meditation, or vegetarian cooking and (better yet) eating. Retreats usually include workshops and educational classes. Some include menus and classes for body detoxification, to cleanse the toxins and stress from everyday life. Retreats like this might include fasting and fitness workouts as well as massage. These vacations tend to cater more toward relaxation and rejuvenation rather than ecological or sustainable travel.

THE GREAT OUTDOORS

National, state, and local parks abound in the United States. A study done by the US Forest Service and the National Oceanic and Atmospheric Administration (NOAA) concluded that thirty-one million people visited national parks for an out-of-doors adventure in 2019. Parks have a lot to offer from overnight stays to hiking, biking, and even riding trails. They give individuals and families a chance to reconnect with each other and nature with providing access to outdoor activities that are sometimes just a few yards away.

Many parks offer educational programs and ranger-led tours. Some of the programs may have a fee, while many of the tours such as fire ring sessions, where rangers gather visitors around a campfire and tell stories or give information about the park and its inhabitants, are free. Joining a tour or program allows visitors to learn more about the park and have a chance to meet other vacationers.

The National Park Service

The National Park Service (NPS) comprises more than four hundred natural, cultural, and recreational areas set aside for people to enjoy. The NPS is operated by the Department of the Interior and was created by President Woodrow Wilson in 1916. Formation of the park service actually came after establishment of the first national park; Yellowstone National Park was established in 1872 by President Ulysses S. Grant.

National parks not only allow visitors to witness some of the country's natural wonders—they also protect watersheds and vital elements in biodiversity. Designation as a national park means that no mining or hunting can take place, and timber cannot be removed. The areas are protected as resources, which also makes them popular destination spots. There are areas protected within the NPS that are not duplicated anywhere else.

When visiting a national park, it's important not to feed the wild animals. Animals that are fed not only lose their fear of humans; they also may act more aggressively around people. To avoid an altercation, keep food stored where it won't be tempting to the animals. Park areas may get overcrowded, especially during July and August. When crowds aren't handled well, parks end up with traffic jams, noise pollution, and poor air quality. Yosemite National Park, which hosts over three million visitors a year, became the first park system to actively pursue a reduction in personal cars. In 2005, the park began operating eighteen 40-foot diesel-electric hybrid buses, encouraging visitors to use the bus system instead of their own vehicles.

As a result, the Environmental and Energy Study Institute reported a 60 percent reduction in nitrogen oxide, a 90 percent reduction in particulate matter, a 70 percent reduction in noise—and an estimated 12,500 gallons of gas saved. Yosemite isn't alone. Many other parks are taking the initiative to ameliorate damages to the environment brought on by their popularity. Years ago, it was thought that increased numbers of visitors meant more exposure, awareness, and enjoyment. This philosophy is being reconsidered as managers try to handle increased visitor numbers with decreased funding.

If you decide to visit a national park, consider going when it's not peak season, or by avoiding peak weekend traffic. There are also a number of beautiful and solitary parks whose only fault is that they are relatively unknown. In any case, you can purchase a national park pass to cover the entrance fee to all national parks; additional fees for camping, parking, or tours are not included.

Check out www.nps.gov for more information.

State Parks

State parks are run by various departments within each state. They offer a variety of camping, hiking, and water activities. Often you can purchase a state pass that allows access to all the parks within a certain state. State parks provide an intriguing alternative to other traditional vacation spots like amusement parks. Not only are nature parks less expensive than amusement parks; they also offer the opportunity to see a little of your own—or someone else's—backyard. Many state parks offer guided tours and even overnight outings. If you'd like to try a new activity but are wary of doing it alone, you may find that joining a tour is the best approach. Experts will be on hand and you will share the company of like-minded folks. Funds generated from these outings usually go back to the park to help with maintenance and maybe even the construction of new facilities.

Many state parks have online reservations available that allow visitors to pick their site and pay online. Schedules and program information are usually available online, so visitors can plan their stay to take advantage of all the park has to offer. To find parks in your state or a state you plan to visit, go to the state's website and run a search.

SIMPLE PLEASURES: YOUR BACKYARD

Not that Dorothy in *The Wizard of Oz* was promoting a greener lifestyle, but her claim that "There's no place like home" often rings true. When eco-friendly time is needed, but time or funds don't allow a full-fledged eco-trip to exotic lands, investigate your own backyard. Local extension offices have information on the kinds of insects or birds you might find nearby. Check out books with a lot of pictures and try to match them with what you see. Some community colleges or outfitters offer classes on local flora and fauna.

Staying close to home gives you the opportunity to get to know the animals that share your yard. If you like them, you can take steps to attract them. Find out what plants grow in your area that will attract birds and butterflies. To attract even more animals, plant a garden and see who comes to visit. Putting up a bird feeder and birdbath will attract feathered friends that are either local to the area or just passing through. Bird counts are a way for residents to watch and tally the different birds that frequent their backyards. If there's a locally organized bird count, enthusiasts can learn even more about the birds in the area throughout the seasons. Outdoor fans may be surprised to find out what kind of endangered species inhabit nearby areas. You can work to help sustain the animal populations. Even if long trips aren't possible, shorter ones may provide just as much fun and excitement.

Nearby city parks can also provide an opportunity to get closer to nature. Parks provide open space for locals to get fresh air and for children to run around and work out their wiggles. Trees help clean the air and provide habitat for birds and squirrels. They offer not just physical relief but visual respite too. Green spaces break up the monotony of structures and roads and offer people a chance to take a breather. There's a chance that local parks and recreation departments are in need of volunteers. By helping park professionals, volunteers are able to learn a lot about their surroundings and the issues they face, from funding to encroachment.

CONCLUSION

Be Like the Buddha and Teach

Teaching others what you have learned on your path to enlightenment is a main tenet of Zen. Sharing your wisdom will help others realize the spiritual bliss and consciousness that comes with green living.

Perhaps the easiest thing in the world to recycle and pass along is information. Learning can be fun and teaching what you've learned can be extremely rewarding. When given the chance, offer a child the opportunity to learn as well, for our youth will be passed the torch of environmental protection.

Remember that Zen is all about the journey and the wisdom that feeds your soul along the way. Being green, the Zen way, means being present and responsible for your personal ripple in the cosmos and the footprint you leave behind you. We have only the now in which to begin, for tomorrow may be too late.

INDEX